Choice Dialogues

Choice Dialogues

A Collection of
New and Original Dialogues
for School and Social
Entertainment

Edited by

Mrs. J. W. SHOEMAKER

Granger Index Reprint Series

BOOKS FOR LIBRARIES PRESS
FREEPORT, NEW YORK

First Published 1888
Reprinted 1970

STANDARD BOOK NUMBER:

8369-6129-3

LIBRARY OF CONGRESS CATALOG CARD NUMBER:

77-109145

MANUFACTURED
BY
HALLMARK LITHOGRAPHERS, INC.
IN THE U.S.A.

PREFACE.

To meet the wants of an increasing public demand has been the object of the preparation of this volume. Many of the excellent dialogues which have hitherto appeared in print have been so frequently utilized, that the call for something NEW has become loud and urgent.

In procuring material for the book, the greatest care has been taken to secure a widely varied range of topics, characters, and conditions; hence there will be found that which is suited to the wants of the little folks, the older boys and girls, and adults.

Some are grave in character, some sprightly, some broadly humorous, adapted alike to the needs of the home, the school-room, the literary society, and the social circle.

With such dialogues as are more difficult in stage setting, or in which the manifestations of character are not clearly defined, full explanations have been given in order to facilitate the work of preparation.

iii

Every appearance of irreverance and every sugges-
tion of coarseness has been carefully excluded, so that
the moral tone of the book, no less than its literary and
artistic merits, may secure for it that high place in the
public estimation which it has been our conscientious
aim in its preparation to reach.

Mrs. J. W. Shoemaker.

CONTENTS.

SCHOOL AND SOCIAL DIALOGUES.

RUGGLES & CO.

CHARACTERS.

MR. NICHOLAS RUGGLES, head of the firm.
HARRY MITCHELL, an office-boy.
RAGGED TOM," the applewoman's son.

SCENE.—*An office; table in the centre, with pens, ink, and paper upon it; chair behind it, also several chairs about right and left of stage. Harry Mitchell discovered seated on corner of table swinging his legs and holding half a dozen letters in his hand.*

Harry (soliloquizing as he looks over the addresses on the letters).—Ruggles & Co., 29 Bond Street; Messrs. Nicholas Ruggles & Co.; Ruggles & Co.; Mr. Nicholas Ruggles One, two, three, four, five, six letters this morning for the firm. That's for us; but then, you see, I don't open the firm's letters. No, the senior partner does that—Mr. Ruggles, that is I'm only the Co. I must be the Co., for there is no other Co. about. Mr. Ruggles says that those two letters, that " C " and that little " o " at the end of the line, add greatly to the effect on the general public—give weight to the house, and all that, you know. He says he don't mind my calling myself the Co., provided it don't make me too proud to be office-boy and sweep out the place, build the fire, wind the clock, and run the errands. Well, I don't think it will. I don't mind working. Mr. Ruggles says it

7

I work very hard and am a good boy and save my money, some day I may be the Co. in earnest, and share the firm's profits. And they're big, they are. [*Referring to the letters, which he still holds.*] These are orders, every one of 'em—orders for our watches—the best watches made for the money. "Warranted to keep seventieth meridian time so well that it can never get away from you." That's what Mr. Ruggles says. He's promised that I can have one when I save up ten dollars—have a real, genuine, eigh-teen dollar, wholesale, silver hunting-case, patent lever, full-jeweled, stem-winder when I save ten dollars; and I've got nine dollar and fifty cents now. Fifty cents more, only fifty cents, Harry Mitchell, and you can carry a watch in your pocket that will————. [*Footsteps are heard outside. Harry springs down from table. Straightens pens, etc., and places letters under a paper-weight.*] It's Mr. Ruggles, I suppose. Wonder what's bringing him down so early this morning! Fully fifteen minutes ahead of time, and he's usually as punctual to the minute as the hands on the watches he sells.

(*Enter Ragged Tom, shivering, and looking pale, hungry, and generally forlorn.*)

Tom (*rubbing his hands*).—By jiminy, aint it cold, though! Can I come in awhile and git warm?

Harry.—Can you? Why of course you can. Take a seat over the register and toast your toes. You look half frozen, sure enough.

(*Ragged Tom comes forward, seats himself on a chair, and hangs his feet over imaginary register.*)

Tom.—That's jolly, that is. [*Still rubbing his hands.*] I haven't been warm for two days, I haven't, and poor mother is almost frozen to death up in our old attic. I wish I could take some of this heat home to her.

Harry.—I wish you could, for we've enough and to spare here, I'm sure. What's your name?

Tom.—Ragged Tom, they call me. Mother's name's Mrs. Mackin. Kitty—Old Kitty—some people call her. She used to sell apples down here in the doorway of this building till she got down with the rheumatism. Since then she hasn't been able to get out. Now she's got the fever, and I'm afraid she's going to die; it's so cold up in our garret.

Harry.—Why don't you move?

Tom.—It would kill her to move her, they say, and besides, we haven't any money—not enough to get a fire or a crust to eat even, let alone pay for a doctor. We're in a bad way, we are. I've tried so hard for work, too, but I can't get it, and when I beg I get cursed at and laughed at, and told to be off and work for money, as other boys have to do.

Harry.—I'm sorry for you, Tom.

Tom.—Are you?

Harry.—That I am! And I want to help you.

Tom.—Oh! will you? If you could only save mother's life.

Harry.—I will if I can. I'm not rich, Tom, but I've got enough to get you a fire and something to eat, and enough to pay for a doctor to see your mother and give her some medicine. Kitty and I used to be great friends, we did, when she kept the apple-stand, and many a time she's given me an apple when I was hungry and hadn't a cent to pay for it. I'm not going to forget her now. [*Aside,*] No, not if I don't get my watch for ten years to come, I won't.

Tom (*jumping up and clapping his hands*).—Oh! how good you are! And have you really got money to do all this?

Harry.—I've saved up a little—nine dollars and a half. It's not much, to be sure, but what there is you and your mother shall have it, every penny! I was going to buy a watch.

Tom.—I'll pay you some day. If mother only gets well I can black boots or sell papers or something, and I'll give you all I earn till I've paid you.

Harry.—Every minute is precious, isn't it? Mr. Ruggles has my money locked up in the drawer there or you should have it now, Tom. But then he won't be long coming. If you're warm enough, suppose you run off after a doctor and send him to your mother. Tell him that Ruggles & Co.—Nicholas Ruggles & Co., that is— wish him to go. I'll foot the bill.

Tom.—What is your name?

Harry.—I'm the Co.—Harry Mitchell, they call me— but you needn't say that to the doctor. Do you see, Tom? Hurry off now, and then come straight back and I'll have some money for you.

Tom.—You're awful good, you are, Harry Mitchell, Mr. Co., or whatever your name is, and mother and I won't forget you, we won't.

(*Exit Tom hurriedly. Harry resumes his place on the corner of the table and begins soliloquizing again.*)

Harry.—Well, I'm not quite so near the watch as I thought I was; but then I couldn't see that little chap starve, and his mother—dear old Kitty, who has been so kind to me—die just because I wanted to be a swell and carry a ticker. Oh! no. Maybe I'm a bad boy! Maybe I am, but I'm not so bad as that, not by a large majority I'm not. [*Noise of footsteps outside again.*] Ah, here comes Mr. Ruggles for certain. [*Jumps down from table just as Mr. Ruggles enters.*]

Mr. Ruggles.—Ah, there you are! I want you to go an errand immediately. Get your hat quick now, and be off. Here's a note [*taking letter from his pocket*] which must be delivered to Mr. Robinson down in the Exchange building before nine o'clock, and it's five minutes of that time now. Off you go! [*Harry picks up his hat from a chair, takes the letter, and stops in front of Mr. Ruggles, who has seated him-self at the table.*]

Harry.—Before I go, sir, won't you please give me—

Mr. R.—I'll give you nothing. Off with you, sir; quick now, and not another word.

(*Harry puts on his hat and makes his exit.*)

Mr. R.—What on earth did that boy want? Maybe I was a little harsh with him, but business is business, and there was no time to lose. Wanted his nine dollars and a half probably. Got tired of saving to buy a watch, I suppose, and wants to invest in a half dozen dime novels, a revolver, a dirk-knife, and go West. Just like a boy. They're all the same; though I did think Harry was a little better than the average. [*Begins opening his letters. Opens each in turn, glances at them, and spreads them out beside him. Takes up pen and commences to write. As he does so, the door opens and Ragged Tom pokes his head in. Mr. Ruggles looks up.*] No, we don't want any matches!

Tom.—I'm not selling matches, sir; I'm—

Mr. R.—Shoe blacking, shoe laces, needles, pins, button-fasteners, soap, lead pencils, etc., all the same; we don't want any.

Tom (*coming further in*).—I haven't anything to sell, sir; I came to—

Mr. R.—Came to beg, did you? Well, we don't give to beggars. We belong to several Soup Societies and all our money for charity goes that way. Get out now. Don't you see I'm busy.

Tom.—But, sir, I was to call back to see the boy—Co, he called himself, or something like that.

Mr. R.—Oh! you want to see the Company do you? Ha! ha! That's a good one. And what do you want to see the little chap for, eh?

Tom.—Please, sir, he promised to pay for a doctor for my mother, who is sick, and to get us some coal and something to eat.

Mr. R.—Who promised you all this?

Tom.—The boy who called himself Co. I think he said some people call him Harry.

Mr. R.—Ah! ha! So he's going to spend his savings on you, is he? Well, if you're worthy of it I don't know but that I admire his generosity. You know he had saved that money to buy himself a watch, don't you?

Tom.—He said something like that, sir; but indeed I'll pay it all back to him—every cent—as soon as I can get work.

Mr. R.—And you want work, do you?

Tom.—Oh! yes, sir; very much.

Mr. R.—And would you be a good boy, and attend to business if I gave you a position here?

Tom.—Oh! wouldn't I, though!

(*Sounds of footsteps outside again.*)

Mr. R.—Sit down over there then, and keep very still while I attend to the Co.

(*Tom sits down. Enter Harry.*)

Mr. R. (*sharply*).—Come here, sir. [*Harry walks to side of table.*] So you have determined to give away your hard earned savings, have you?

Harry.—I thought this poor boy and his mother needed it so much more than I did.

Mr. R.—Very well, then, you shall have it; but how about your watch?

Harry.—Oh! I can get along without that for a time yet, sir.

Mr. R.—You can, can you? Well I think differently. You can't, as the tail end of this firm, get along without one. To tell the truth, young man, I'm not altogether satisfied with you as an errand boy, and this action of yours has determined me to relieve you. Your services as errand boy are no longer required.

Harry.—O Mr Ruggles! I hope you won't—

Mr. R.—Not a word, sir. I have spoken. Your place is already filled. That youth on the chair there is to be your successor.

Harry.—Am I discharged then, Mr. Ruggles?

Mr. R.—Discharged! Not a bit of it, my boy; not a bit of it. I wouldn't think of discharging a lad with a heart as big as yours. You will be a member of the firm in earnest some day, Harry. For the present, you are to be my clerk. You write a good hand, and you're getting too big to run errands. As I said, however, you can't get along without a watch; so I'm going to give you one. And I'm going to do something for you [*turning to Ragged Tom*]. You had better stop with your mother until she is better and then you can come and take Harry's place. Tell me where you live, and Ruggles & Co.—that's Harry and I—will fix you up. [*Taking bills from his pocket.*] Meanwhile, take this—it's the junior member's money—and see that your mother is comfortable.

(*Tom takes money and Harry, smiling, begins to thank Mr. Ruggles.*)

Harry.—O sir! you are too good, Mr. Ruggles. I thank you more than I—

Tom.—And I thank you too, sir!

Mr. R.—Never mind the thanks, boys. Wish the firm success, that's all!

Tom and Harry (in chorus).—We do! We do!

Mr. Ruggles.—Give three cheers for Ruggles & Co.!

Tom and Harry (shouting).—Hurrah! Hurrah! Hurrah! Success to Ruggles & Co.!

[CURTAIN.]

CHARLES STOKES WAYNE.

THE GODS IN COUNCIL.

CHARACTERS AND COSTUMES.

JUPITER, white chiton, purple drapery, golden staff.

JUNO, white chiton, cardinal drapery, short golden staff, and crown.

MARS, white chiton, cardinal drapery, helmet, shield, staff in form of spear all three silver.

NEPTUNE, green drapery, a silver trident and crown.

PLUTO, black chiton, yellow drapery, wooden scepter, yellow crown.

MINERVA, white chiton, blue drapery, silver helmet, shield, and spear.

APOLLO, white chiton, blue drap·ry, golden lyre.

VULCAN, white chiton, black drapery, hammer.

VESTA, white chiton, white drapery.

DIANA, cream-colored drapery, silver bows and arrows, with quiver at her back.

CERES, white chiton, pink drapery, crown of cereals on her head, a lighted torch in her hand.

MERCURY, long gray stockings, short gray drapery streaming behind him, winged cap and sandals, caduceus.

(Shawls can be used to good effect in the drapery, while shields, spears, etc., can be made of wood or pasteboard and covered with gold or silver paper.)

(Enter Jupiter and Mercury from one side, and Juno from the other.)

Juno (addressing Jupiter).—My lord, do the gods assemble to-day in council?

Jupiter (turning to Mercury).—Mercury, go thou through the corridors of Olympus and summon the gods to council.

(Mercury bows and flies to do his bidding. Enter some of the deities at one door, some at the other, and group themselves about Jupiter, who is seated on his throne.)

Jupiter.—Give ear, all ye gods and goddesses, while I declare the thought within my breast. Let none of either sex presume to sit in this last divine council of the gods, without broad ideas, piercing thought, grave emotions and eloquent words.

Now, what shall be the issue of the present state of affairs in heaven and among mortals? This is the question: Shall the gods try to regain their former relations to man and be worshiped throughout the earth or not?

Ye dwellers of the sky, in answering this question, first consider the great achievements of man incumbered by the dark clay of the earth, and then the ability of the gods in the freedom of space.

Know ye now, that I shall weigh your thoughts in the "scale of justice," and as the argument goes, so shall be the eternal conclusion of affairs.

(Turning to Juno.) What think you, most wise goddess and queen of the heavens?

Juno.—As queen of all the gods and mistress of heaven and earth, I would regain my former power. It would be my greatest pleasure, as of old, to guard woman against tyranny and aid her in the assertion of her rights. I would crown her untiring efforts, made through the long centuries, with victory, participating in her final triumph. The golden apple, though bestowed upon another, would no longer excite my envy. Because of man's increased appreciation of the talents and ability of woman, my powers as a goddess would no longer be undervalued, and all cause for jealousy would cease.

Pluto.—Ye gods, " great in action and in council wise,"

once was I dire monarch in the kingdom of the lost, but
since the usurpation of my throne the cry of the oppressed
sounds to mine ear from under the oppressor's fiery heel.
Their cry doth rend my heart, and shall I idly listen to
their wail?

By Styx! I mean this tyrant's reign shall end; and the
fast increasing subjects of Hades shall rise to welcome
Pluto's just and lawful reign. Awake, O Gods!

> " Why would ye bid to shun the coming fight?
> And would ye move to base, inglorious flight?
> Know ye, 'tis not honest in your soul to fear."

In time of old we reigned supreme, and all were subject
to our power; and shall we sleep while puny man with his
inventions of these latter days defies our might?

Up then, ye gods, and with united strength we will regain the kingdoms that rightfully are ours.

Neptune.—Most high and mighty Jupiter, who alone of
all these is greater than I, it is to thee I address my argument on this grave subject.

Three thousand years ago the oceans and rivers were
mine. The mountains and forests trembled as I walked.
With a blow of my trident I raised islands out of the deep,
and caused earthquakes at my pleasure.

But, Jupiter, my old haunts are broken up; the whales
and dolphins no longer gambol about me; my daughters
are driven from their caves and grottoes. The discerning
intellect of man has found the history of all our former
greatness in natural laws. The Inmans, the Allans, and
the Cunarders plow the mighty ocean with no thought of
Poseidon to aid their swiftness, and no fear of his wrath.
In view of all this, I find

"All things invite to peaceful counsels and a settled state
Of order. Now in safety best we may
Compose our present evils, with regard
Of what we are and were; dismissing quite
All thoughts of war."

Mars.--Great Jupiter, why need I wish for the power
and rule of old, when I stop and reflect that in my youth
nearly the whole ambition of the people was to prepare
for war. A Spartan entered his public career as a soldier
at the age of seven, and continued such until he was sixty;
but now, how is it? Instead of gaining fame by excelling
in brave deeds and daring exploits, they seek to build up
their fame with what they call the finer arts, such as music,
painting, and poetry. When they do enter into conflict, it
is not, as it used to be, power against power, but skill against
skill; by the invention of powder the weakest man in the
whole army can put into execution the most cruel man-
destroyer ever invented.

No, Jupiter, with these conditions of affairs, I could do
nothing, and would not even wish to have again the power
and rule I once held over the kingdom of mankind.

Minerva.—O Father Jove and all ye blessed ones who
live forever, let our sceptered King be gracious, mild, and
merciful toward the mortal race. We know thy power is
not to be withstood, yet are we moved with pity for the
people made in our own image. Such has been their ad-
vancement in the art and science of war, that, presumptu-
ously relying on their unaided wisdom, they will not fear
a combat even with celestial beings—a combat which to
them must end in an evil fate.

Why arouse them to their own destruction, O son of
Saturn! since then, alas! would there be none left to pay us

homage? Let us rather trust that misguided man, led by his convictions and inherited sense of what is due to us as immortal beings, may of his own free will return to his former allegiance and worship. This is the counsel of Minerva once in men's eyes the queen of wisdom, great and powerful, and adored as the patroness and teacher of all just and scientific warfare, the instructress of every skillful artist.

Vulcan.—So long have we rested peacefully from our cares, I do not desire to again be placed upon earth to repeat the toils and labors which it was my lot to undergo. We have reigned supreme as gods of the earth; we, the mighty have fallen; we are cast from our spheres and only war and desolation can restore us.

O, valiant gods and goddesses of excellency, brave and faithful to the last; though overpowered, yet we are triumphant, for our honor will never die. Blest and glorious be thy name and race, O brave and honored Jupiter! I am wearied with the anvil and hammer, so long have I wielded the strong and mighty strokes that forged the heavy thunderbolts of Jove, and now I long for rest.

Vesta.—I am Vesta, the home goddess. I had ever a pure and uplifting influence on the soul of man, and every hearthstone was consecrated to my worship. I would that I had my power back again, for then would I keep men from all evil! I would strive to teach them the true path of life and make them true and faithful to their duties and loving toward all mankind.

Apollo.—All powerful Jupiter, son of Saturn, mightiest among the potentates in this most august assembly of the gods and goddesses, Phœbus Apollo speaks in favor of war. Let us arise in our might and compel these weak and presumptuous people to acknowledge our supremacy.

There was a time, most august father, when men were

much more warlike than at present, that one of their most illustrious poets exclaimed, " Who is so rash as to resist the gods?" It is in the power of the gods to prove that they have indeed been rash.

Let Vulcan forge for each a suit of armor, and whilst Mars is shaking the earth with his thunder and thou art hurling thunderbolts of wrath upon their heads, the rest of the gods and goddesses will descend and drive them all into the dark regions of Hades. This we might have accomplished long ago had we united our efforts. Therefore let us not delay, but descend at once, for Phœbus Apollo will never tune this divine lyre, until the authority of the immortal gods and goddesses is established forever.

Ceres.—O blessed of heaven! thou askest Ceres whether she would regain her former rule.

Once all earth smiled when I smiled, and wept when I wept; but what availed my power? Vainly I spread mine earthly fruits and flowers. She became another's, who was once my child, Persephone. She left with scarce a sigh her mother's care to hold his [*gesture toward Pluto*] sceptre and his kingdom share!

And yet, great Jove! were it for the good of suffering humanity, I would e'en take up again the power which now is only mockery; but men are not as they were; they reap wealth by preying on their fellows. If I should seek to reward the virtuous by increasing the harvests, I would simply expose them to the cupidity and rapaciousness of the wicked. Therefore, O Father Jove, am for peace.

Diana.—During my reign upon the earth, I chose the woods for my dominion and the chase for my occupation I delighted to wander through the forests attended by my maidens, where grew the fennel green and balm and golden pines, savory, lattermint and columbines, cool parsley, basil sweet and sunny thyme.

Yea, every flower and leaf of every clime we gathered in the dewy morning. Our great labor, however, was to slay the wild boar and wolves which infested the forests, and which were the much-dreaded enemies of man.

I had other work besides that of a huntress to perform. I was queen of the moon, and nightly, unobserved, I stole away to my throne, sending my clear, silvery rays to pierce the darkness of the earth, and by the light of my bright tapers I often saw my maidens dancing on the dewy grass.

But, during the hundreds of centuries that I have been absent from the earth, the human race has so increased, both in numbers and power, that they have been obliged to fell the forests, and have been enabled to exterminate the wild beasts. So that now I have no desire to return to the earth, as the scenes of my former labors have been obliterated.

Mercury.—Father Jove, although but the messenger of the gods, I think I should have something to say on this question.

For many years I held supreme power as messenger, but now I feel that my occupation is indeed gone. Now electricity and steam outdistance me, and I wish to retire and leave puny man, as he has been here styled, in full possession.

Therefore, ye gods, let us not attempt to regain our power, but retire to peace and everlasting rest.

Jupiter.—Gods and goddesses, I thank you for the wise counsel that has proceeded from your lips; but for my own thought, I may say this: it is below the grandeur and greatness of the gods to take any offensive stand against the inhabitants of the earth. They themselves are conscious of the narrow limits of their ability and understanding. They to-day may stand in defiance of all that is noble and higher than themselves, but the hard problems of life are before them, and as soon as their frail natures are defeated they will again offer sacrifices at the altars of the immortal gods, hoping for guidance and strength.

Therefore I declare that none of us shall make any effort to regain the confidence of man. You may now return to the inactivity which you have followed for the past eighteen hundred years. [*Exit all.*]

Arranged by EMILY RADCLIFF.

ALMOST A MORMON.

CHARACTERS.

JOHN MANLY, a Yankee, resident of Salt Lake City.
MRS. MANLY, his wife.
ALICE SINCLAIR, on a visit to Utah.
ARTHUR MAYTON, her lover.
TOMMY, ⎫
SALLIE,   ⎬ children of the Manlys.
JERUSHA, ⎭

SCENE.—*A neatly furnished living room. Lounge at right,
table in centre, chairs at back; also chair and two stools at
left. Curtain rises, disclosing Mrs. Manly bending over
Miss Sinclair, who lies upon lounge apparently asleep. Tom-
mie, Sallie and Jerusha seated on chairs and stools at right.*

Mrs. Manly.—There now, she's asleep! Dear me! dear
me! How innocent she looks, to be sure! To think that
she should want to come here and take half of my John's
love from me and his children. O the huzzy. What
a mask that face is! No wonder she's nervous and frightened. She ought to be nervous, and if it wasn't she is so
frail and delicate looking I'd give her reason to be frightened, too. [*Turning to the children.*] Ah, my little dears!
Aren't you ashamed of your father? To think that he has
so far forgotten you as to want to give you another mother!
As if one mother was not enough to scold you when you
are naughty and to pet you when you are good. Did you
want another mother, my dears?

Children.—No, ma'am!

Mrs. Manly.—Of course you didn't, and he ought to have
considered your wishes and mine, too. Did I not tell him
when we came out here from New England that the first
thing that happened he would be adopting these Mormon
ideas and practicing polygamy?

22

Children.—Yes, ma'am!

Mrs. Manly.—And what did he say to me? Didn't he tell me that he hated the very idea of Mormonism; that I was all the wife he wanted, and too much sometimes, and that he only came here because he could earn more money here than he could East. Didn't he?

Children.—Yes, ma'am!

Mrs. Manly.—And to think that he should so soon forget his promises! O John Manly! John Manly! How could you? "Do you expect me to love her?" I asked him when he brought her in here ten minutes ago, and to think that he had the impudence to say, "Yes! yes! Be good to her; try to get her to sleep. She is very nervous; the elder frightened her." Did you hear him say that, children?—"The elder frightened her?"

Children.—Yes, ma'am!

Mrs. Manly.—Do you know what that meant?

Children.—No, ma'am!

Mrs. Manly.—It meant that your father has had this woman sealed to him—sealed by the elders. That means married, my dears! She is your father's wife in the sight of the Mormons just as much as I am. More so, I guess, because no Mormon elder sealed me, but a good dominie in a Connecticut meeting house, and these Mormons don't much believe in dominies any more than the dominies believe in the Mormons.

Tommy.—Where has papa gone now? To get another mother for us?

Mrs. Manly.—Well, I hope not! You don't suppose he's going into the business wholesale, do you? Don't you think two wives are enough for any man, and more than enough?

Children (in chorus).—Yes, ma'am!

Mrs. Manly.—Your father, my dears, has gone for a doctor for his second wife, I suppose. She's going to begin to run up doctor's bills already and rob you of what property belongs to you. You don't like that much, do you?

Children.—No, ma'am!

Mrs. Manly.—No, of course you don't. It means you must go without any new shoes this spring, Tommy; and you, Sallie, must do without the new frock you ought to have; and you, Jerusha, must wear that faded sunbonnet another season.

Children.—Yes, ma'am!

Mrs. Manly.—Oh! it's terrible! terrible!

(*Miss Sinclair moves on lounge and opens her eyes.*)

Mrs. Manly.—There, my dears, your new mother is waking. Do you see her?

Children.—Yes, ma'am!

Mrs. Manly (*to Miss Sinclair*).—Do you feel better, madam?

Miss Sinclair (*raising herself on her elbow*).—Madam, did you say? I am no madam, I am Miss Sinclair.

Mrs. Manly.—Excuse me, but you are not. Maybe you were an hour ago, but you're sealed now, and you're a miss no longer.

Miss Sinclair (*jumping up suddenly*).—O do not say that! Where am I?

Mrs. Manly.—At your husband's home, under his roof, in the care of his wife!

Miss Sinclair.—But this is outrageous! I—

Mrs. Manly.—What is outrageous? You don't mean to say this home is not good enough for you! If it's good enough for John Manly's first wife, it's certainly good enough for his second.

Miss Sinclair.—But I'm not his wife. I'm—

Mrs. Manly.—You're not his wife! [*To children.*] Do you hear that, my dears? She's not his wife! Oh, my dear lady, you're wandering; your mind's affected.

Miss Sinclair.—No, I am quite rational. I had a severe nervous attack just now. I'm subject to them, but I've quite recovered, and I can assure you that I am not his wife. I was visiting the Tabernacle and I got into conversation with him. I said I thought I would like to be a Mormon. I said it just in a joke, you know, when he threw his arms about me and said I should be. He had looked with favor upon me, and he would seal me unto him.

Mrs. Manly.—O the villain! John, my husband, how could you so far forget your promises of loyalty to me!

Miss Sinclair.—But he could not marry me against my will.

Mrs. Manly.—O that makes no difference. The Mormon elders don't mind trifles like that. There's no getting over it. You're his wife and no mistake and I suppose you'll have to make the best of it, just as we are making the best of it. Won't she, children?

Children.—Yes, ma'am!

Miss Sinclair.—O horror! This is outrageous! Is there no law in Utah?

Mrs. Manly.—The law of the Book of Mormon, that's about all.

Miss Sinclair.—But, my friends, I have an uncle at the hotel, and a cousin. I will go to them at once. [*Getting up and starting for door at left.*]

Mrs. Manly.—I wish I could aid you; but I daresay you will not go far. Your husband has probably posted a sentinel outside of the door. Don't you think so, children?

Children.—Yes, ma'am!

Miss Sinclair.—But I shall try! There is no harm in trying. O I must escape!

(*Miss Sinclair is about to go out when there is a knock at the door, L. She starts back in affright and sinks into a chair.*)

Mrs. Manly.—Who on earth is that? [*Going to door and opening it.*]

(*Enter Arthur Mayton.*)

Arthur.—Is this where Mr. Manly lives?

Mrs. Manly.—Yes, sir.

Arthur.—And is this Mrs. Manly?

Mrs. Manly.—One of 'em, sir.

Arthur.—I have come to—

Miss Sinclair (*starting up*).—O Arthur! Arthur!

Arthur (*pushing past Mrs. Manly*).—Alice, my darling! I am so glad to find you. [*Is about to embrace her when Mrs. Manly speaks.*]

Mrs. Manly.—Hands off, sir! Are you not ashamed of yourself, sir? How dare you put your hands on another man's wife!

Arthur (*turning and facing Mrs. Manly*).—Another man's wife! What do you mean, madam?

Mrs. Manly.—I mean that that young lady has been sealed to John Manly by the Mormon Church, that she is his wife, and that she is now half mother and third owner of these children. [*To children.*] Is she not, my dears?

Children.—Yes, ma'am!

Arthur.—Nonsense! This is preposterous! Why, it has only been a few hours since she left us at the hotel to go on an independent tour of inspection of Salt Lake City and its Mormon Tabernacle.

Mrs. Manly.—And the Mormons have claimed her.

Miss Sinclair.—O Arthur, take me away! This seems like some horrid dream; it cannot be real.

Arthur.—To be sure I'll take you away. Come!

(*Enter John Manly hurriedly.*)

Mrs. Manly.—You are just in time, John!

John.—In time for what?

Arthur.—In time to explain your conduct, sir! That's what you are in time for.

Mrs. Manly.—Yes, and in time to defend yourself before me, your wife, and those [*pointing to children*], your off-spring! O John Manly! How could you do this thing?

John.—I have done nothing that I would not do again and again, whenever occasion offered.

Arthur (*aside*).—The hardened wretch!

Mrs. Manly.—O you awful Mormon! What do you suppose your dominie at home would say if he heard you say that?

John.—Say well done, I suppose.

Miss Sinclair.—Who is this?

Mrs. Manly.—Your husband, of course; don't you know him?

John.—What? Her husband! Who's her husband?

Mrs. Manly.—Why, you, aren't you?

John.—I? Not much. As I have said before, one wife is enough, and sometimes more than enough, for me. Don't accuse me of being a Mormon. I hate 'em.

Arthur.—Then you did not attempt to make this young lady your wife?

John.—Well, hardly! One wife and the children there are all I can support.

Mrs. Manly.—Then maybe you will explain your conduct that you are so willing to repeat.

John.—I will in very few words. I happened to be passing the Tabernacle this afternoon when I saw Elder Slabback. You know the old wretch, my dear—the fellow who winked at you the first Sunday we were in Salt Lake. Well, as I said, I saw him carrying this young lady out of the Tabernacle. He had her up in his arms like a baby. " Where are you going ?" I asked. " That is my business," he replied. A little shaver who happened by spoke up. " I saw him in the Tabernacle," he said ; " he wanted to seal the girl to him, and she said she wouldn't have it. Then she fainted, and he carried her off. I guess he's going to seal her." With that I followed the Elder and told him to take her back to the hotel. [*To Miss Sinclair.*] I saw your face, miss, and remembered having seen you at the hotel. He refused, and told me to be off. Then I had a tussle with him, got the best of him, rescued you, and hurried you over here. You recovered from the faint and had a fit of hysterics on the way here, and I thought it best to leave you in my wife's care while I hurried to the hotel for your friends.

Miss Sinclair.—O how good of you !

Arthur.—You're a noble fellow. Let me thank you !

(*Arthur and John shake hands.*)

John.—When I got to the hotel I tried to explain whom I wanted ; but, as I didn't know your names, I couldn't make the stupid clerk understand.

Arthur.—And I had just stepped out, having become nervous about Miss Sinclair's absence. I heard people talking about a fellow named Manly having carried a young lady into his cottage. I inquired where it was and came straight here.

Mrs. Manly.—O my brave husband ! I'm as proud of

you as though you had been elected to Congress and had a bill passed abolishing Mormonism.

Arthur.—That may come in time. Mr. Manly has begun well, certainly.

Mrs. Manly.—And the children are proud of him, too, aren't you, my dears?

Children.—Yes, ma'am!

Miss Sinclair.—And then I am not married after all, and, Mrs. Manly, I am still a miss?

Mrs. Manly.—Yes, miss; but it looks very much to me [*looking sharply at Arthur, who has his arm about her*] that you won't be a miss long.

Arthur.—Not if I can help it, Mrs. Manly.

Mrs. Manly.—Well, we wish you joy! Don't we, John?

John.—We do, that's certain!

Mrs Manly (to children).—Don't we, my dears?

Children.—Yes, ma'am!

[CURTAIN.]

CHARLES STOKES WAYNE.

BRIDGET'S INVESTMENT.

CHARACTERS.

BRIDGET, a servant.
MRS. MORGAN, her employer.
BOY, a stove-polish vender.
GENTLEMAN.
AN AGENT, selling tea.

SCENE I.

Bridget ironing and humming a tune. Enter Mrs. Morgan.

Mrs. M.—Bridget, I am going out for a few hours, and I shall expect you to finish the ironing while I'm out. You can do it easily if you have no interruptions. Don't let any of those nuisances—traveling agents or peddlers keep you from your work.

Bridget.—Sure, and I won't. If any of the botherin' chates attimpts to shtop within, I'll shlap to the door in their impident faces, or give them a bit of me moind, afther which they'll be deloighted to lave me in pace.

Mrs. M.—Very well. I'll be home at two. [*Exit.*]

Bridget.—The misthress doesn't know Biddy Muldoon if she thinks I'll be tuk in by one of thim peddlin' chates. I'm just sp'ilin' for a chance till relave my tongue by sassin' thim, and its meself wishes one of thim would come. [*A knock is heard.*] Fwhat was that? A knock? I'll go to the door and say. [*Opens the door, and a voice is heard.*]

Boy.—Want any stove-polish? Make your stove or range shine like a lookin'-glass, so as ye can see your purty face in it.

Bridget.—Be off wid ye's. Your blarneyin' tongue won't sell ye's any stove-polish here the day.

Boy.—But, can't I—

Bridget.—Git out, will ye's, now, before I'll be afther callin' the dog. [*Shuts the door, comes in, and goes on ironing and humming the tune, but is interrupted by another knock.*] Whisht, now! There's another. Sorra a bit will me ironin' git complated wid me runnin' to the door ivery foive minutes. [*Goes to the door and shouts.*] We don't want anything the day. We're complately shupplied wid shoe-blackin', castile soap, sewin' machines, oranges and limons, patent egg-beaters, hangin' hat-racks, and appoortenances ginerally. Ye's can't sell me the amount of a tinpint-pace, and ye's may as well waltz off the door-steps.

Gentleman.—But, my good girl, I'm not asking you to buy anything. I merely called to see Mrs. Morgan on a matter of business.

Bridget.—The misthress is gone out, but she will be home at two o'clock, axin' your pardon for me mistakin ye's for an agent.

Gentleman.—I'll call again. Good-morning.

Bridget.—Good-morning, sir. [*Closing the door and again ironing.*] It's meself that got a holt of the wrong ind of the iron that time. Mistakin' a gintleman for a peddler! It all comes of the misthress's care in cautionin' me about the agents. But this shirrut looks foine and smooth, now doesn't it. Siven shirruts a week for one mon. The masther must be very dirthy to make so much washin' and ironin'. There is Pat O'Rourke, now. Pat can wear a shirrut thray wakes widout changin'. Pat's a foine b'y, so he is. [*A knock is heard.*] Bad luck till the door-knocker! There it goes again. Sure, I'll kape me tongue in me mouth this toime, till I say fwhat is wanted, and not be gettin' meself into a foine blunder again.

(*Goes to the door and opens it.*)

Agent.—Ah! good-morning, madam. Have I the pleasure of addressing the lady of the house ?

Bridget.—Sorra a bit have ye's.

Agent.—Ah! A lady friend staying with her, I presume.

Bridget.—Ye's preshume more than the facts will warrant ye's in preshuming. Fwhat are ye's afther wantin' ?

Agent.—I'll just step in a minute out of the damp air, and then we can converse in comfort. [*Walks boldly in.*] I hope I don't intrude, as I would not on any account incommode a lady who has received a stranger so kindly. [*Looks around the room with a patronizing air.*] Very pleasant room this is, worthy of its occupant. [*Bowing politely to Bridget.*] It needs but one thing to make it perfect.

Bridget (*evidently pleased*).—And fwhat moight that be!

Agent.—An instrument of music, to be sure. I see by the shape of your hands—those long, taper fingers—that you are, or ought to be, a musician.

Bridget.—I can't say, as I'm a complate performer at prisent, but, as Pat O'Rourke fraquently tells me, niver have I seen the undertakin' as was too hard for me whin I thried it.

Agent.—And wouldn't you like to have a nice cottage-organ of your own?

Bridget.—Faix, and I would that!

Agent.—I am an agent, representing a large tea warehouse in the city, and we wish to extend our business. Of course, to do that, we offer extra inducements to buyers. Any one purchasing to the amount of ten pounds of tea at seventy-five cents a pound will receive an organ as a premium. Isn't that an easy way to get a musical instrument?

Bridget.—Faith, an' ye's can't be in airnest!

Agent.—I certainly mean it. No such inducements were ever offered to purchasers before, but there is no sham about it. Purchase the tea and the organ will arrive in the course of a few hours.

Bridget.—Tin toimes sivinty-five cents is—

Agent.—Seven dollars and fifty cents, ma'am.

Bridget.—And have ye's the tay wid ye's?

Agent.—Certainly, madam. It is here, in this package. Just ten pounds in the package, done up in one-pound parcels.

Bridget.—Perhaps I'd betther be waitin' till I shpakes wid the misthress.

Agent.—Of course I would not wish you to buy unless you feel perfectly satisfied that all is fair and square. Our firm is a reliable one. It is because we do business on such a large scale that we can afford to make these presents. I wouldn't wait to see the lady, if I were you. Perhaps she will be jealous of you and wish to get the organ herself. You had better secure it. This [*getting up and selecting a place in the room*] would be just the place for it to stand. How I wish you had it now. I would so delight to hear you play and sing.

Bridget.—And will the organ be here the day?

Agent.—Before night, madam.

Bridget.—But fwhat will I do wid all that tay? [*Laughing.*] Faix, and I can make prisents to all me frinds and relations—

Agent.—Besides having enough to go to housekeeping along with Pat—the lucky fellow!

Bridget.—Arrah! how did ye's know about Pat?

Agent.—Never mind, I do know, and a happy man he'll be with his nice little wife.

Bridget.—Git away wid ye's now! Here, I'll take the tay, and pay ye's the price of it. It's all good luck that made me ax the misthress for me money this mornin'. [*Gets her purse, and counts out the money.*] There's foive, six, siven dollars, and a quarther, and two tins and a foive. That's correct, I belave.

Agent.—Quite correct, and here is your package of tea. Good-morning. You'll not see me again, as I will not bring the organ myself, but you must not forget me.

Bridget.—Faix, and I'll think of ye's whin I am playin' me own organ, loike any other lady, and good luck be wid ye's. [*Exit agent. Bridget picks up the package.*] Troth, and fwhat a lot of it there is. I can make it foine and shtrong for Pat, sure. But to think of me having an organ of me own. Faith, and I won't be proud; I'll let the misthress show me how to play. [*Exit, carrying package.*]

Scene II.

Bridget (enters with knitting, and glances at the clock).—Siven o'clock is it? And the foine organ not yit arrived. Well, here's the chance to round off the hale of my shtockin' whilst I'm waitin' for it. [*Commences to knit, and hums a line or two of "Kitty Tyrrell," or some other familiar air, then suddenly stops her knitting and finishes the tune, using her hands as though playing on the instrument.*] Och! but won't Pat shtare when he comes in the morrow, and sees me foine iushtrument fornenst the wall, and me, loike my misthress, the lady, playin' the accompaniments and singing the chunes. But whist! here she comes now—the mis-thress, I mane—and I must kape quiet. Time enough to tell her about it when the men are bringin' it in.

Mrs. M. (entering with books and papers).—Well, Bridget, I thought I would bring my book and sit with you awhile. The front part of the house is so lonesome, now that John's away. You finished your ironing to-day, did you?

Bridget.—Faix and I did—as pritty a wake's airnin' as iver ye seed. The collars and cuffs are loike boards, mum, and it would take a stronger person nor you to break in the shirrut bosoms, they are that stiff and firrum loike. [*Glancing uneasily at the window.*]

Mrs. M.—Hadn't you better close the shutters, Bridget? That is, if it makes you nervous to have them open.

Bridget.—Niver a bit, mum. Shure and I loike to give the little shtars a chance to pape in; hark! fwhat was that?

Mrs. M.—I heard nothing unusual, Bridget; some one passing the door, I think. [*Resumes her reading.*]

Bridget (resumes her humming for a moment, then starts up suddenly).—Is that a wagon shtopping at the door?

Mrs. M.—Certainly not. It seems to me, Bridget, your organ—

Bridget.—Och! and do you know about it, then? Where is it? Who told ye? Did ye see the gintleman himself?

Mrs. M.—What in the world are you talking about, Bridget? Where is what? See whom? I was merely remarking that your organ of hearing seems very acute to-night.

Bridget.—Oh-h-h! [*Aside: Wasn't I the doonce to be afther given mysel' away in that stoile.*] Now I know what you mane; shtupid I was not to understand you at first.

Mrs M.—Bridget, there's something on your mind, and you may as well tell me what it is. Have you and Pat had a quarrel, and are you looking for him to come and make up? That you expect some one is very evident.

Bridget.—Yes, Mrs. Morgan, 'tis mysel' that do expect some one, but it isn't Pat. And as you're bound to foind out sometime, I'll tell you fwhat I've been afther doin'. I bargained for an organ the mornin', mum, and sure I'm lookin' ivery minute for the mon what will fetch it here the night.

Mrs. M.—An organ! You buy an organ, Bridget?

Bridget.—Faix, and I didn't buy an organ. It's a pramium for the tay.

Mrs. M.—A premium for what tea?

Bridget.—For the tay I bought the mornin', mum. Such a nice, spry-lookin' young gintleman he was, Mrs. Morgan. He represinted a large tay firrum in the city, he said. "And," says he, "if you will take tin pounds of me tay, I will prisent you wid a handsome organ." "That's a good bargain for me," says I. "If you're afraid it's a risk," said he, "don't ye do it." Wid that I takes out my poorse and counts the money into his hand—siven dollars and fifty cints. And sorra a bit do I grave for the money—it was a chape inshtrument at that, and the tay thrown in.

Mrs. M.—Bridget, Bridget, is it possible that you have been the dupe of that outrageous swindle, which has just been exposed in this evening's paper.

Bridget.—Swindle, do you say?

Mrs. M.—Yes, a swindle.

Bridget.—And won't I get the organ?

Mrs. M.—I'm afraid not. [*Opening the paper.*] Listen to this. [*Reads:*] A young man of good address and pleasing manners, representing himself to be an agent for a large tea warehouse in this city, has been canvassing the country, offering great inducements to purchasers in the way of pianos, sewing-machines, organs, etc. Incredible as it may seem, many persons have been victimized, and the so-called agent has by this time made good his escape.

Bridget.—And do you think that's the same mon as sold me the tay?

Mrs. M.—There's no doubt about it, Bridget.

Bridget.—O the rascal! he desarves to be prosecuted.

Mrs. M.—He's too smart to be caught now, I'm think-ing.

Bridget.—Well, mum, there's one consolation lift me, I have the tay, you know.

Mrs. M.—Suppose you bring it in, Bridget, and let us see what it is like.

Bridget (goes out and returns with the tea, opens the package, and picks up one of the parcels and smells it).—Is it grane or black? I niver moinded me to ax the rascally chate the natur of it. [*Opens it.*] Begorra, I don't belave it's tay at all. Look at it, Mrs. Morgan.

Mrs. M.—It looks to me like dried rose-leaves and shav-ings. O Bridget! you have been sadly duped.

Bridget (opening another).—And this is joost like it. Och, the villain! Wouldn't I like to clutch him now.

Mrs. M.—I think, probably, Bridget, you will find one pound of the real article in your package, as that much is needed to give an odor of tea to the whole; but you have paid dear for it, and I am sorry for you. But, Bridget, you must remember that though the man is a rascal, you are in fault, too. Those who aim to get valuable articles for little or nothing are not blameless. If there were no foolish people, eager to grasp more than they pay for, these dishonest tricksters would find no base for their operations.

Bridget.—Sure, and I know ye's are right, and I'm afther gettin' the retoorn which I merit, but it's no more comfort-abler for all that. I only hopes Pat won't hear of it.

Mrs. M.—We'll try to keep the secret to ourselves. You're sufficiently punished, so I'll keep quiet.

[CURTAIN.]

E. C. AND L. J. ROOK.

TEN FAMOUS WOMEN.

ELEVEN CHARACTERS: The GODDESS OF HISTORY should be attired in a flowing robe, with loose drapery across the chest. She may be seated with five or six good-sized volumes at her feet. In her left hand a partly unrolled manuscript; in her right hand a wand, which she waves to bring forward the different persons represented. The other ten should be dressed to imi-tate the characters they portray. They should stand in a group or semi-circle, and each one as she speaks should step a little to the front, and remain there until the others have recited the verse about her, after which she may return to her place.

Then, if it is deemed necessary, the GODDESS may make known the character by pronouncing the name, or it may be left for the audience to guess
To get a good idea of the proper costumes, consult history and portraits.

Joan of Arc, 1411–1431 :

I was born in a land across the seas, nearly five hundred
years ago. I was the daughter of a humble peasant, and
in my girlhood often tended my father's sheep. But the
land which I loved was invaded by a foreign foe, and the
young King was yet uncrowned. I began to see visions
and dream dreams; and God revealed to me that it was
my mission to lead the armies of my sovereign, and free
my country from the enemy. The young King believed in
me and the soldiers followed me to victory. After my
sovereign was crowned at Rheims, I wished to go back to
my humble home, but he persuaded me to remain with the
army. I was captured by my rebellious countrymen, delivered into the hands of the English, condemned to death
as a sorceress, and burned at the stake. The people were
moved to tears by the heroism with which I met death,
and even my executioner cried out, in an agony of repent-
ance, " We are lost! We have burned a saint!"

All the others in concert :

" Truth forever on the scaffold, wrong forever on the
    throne ;—
But that scaffold sways the future, and, behind the dim
    unknown
Standeth God within the shadow, keeping watch above His
    own."—*Lowell.*

Queen Elizabeth, 1533–1603 :

I was the most powerful sovereign that ever ruled the
greatest nation on the earth. There was never a queen
who had more famous courtiers than I. One of these,

while he was yet unknown to the world, spread his velvet mantle on the ground to keep my royal feet from the stain; another, "the glass of fashion and the mould of form," gave, with his dying breath, a cup of water to a man, whose necessity was greater than his. During my reign the greatest poet flourished that ever wrote to delight mankind; and the strongest fleet that had ever been sent against any nation was driven back, dismantled, from my country's shores. Mine was not the mere semblance of glory, for in reality, as well as in name, I lived and died a queen.

All the others :

> Men say that woman cannot rule,
>   That hers is only to obey ;
> But unto thee men bent the knee,
>   And England owned thy legal sway,

Josephine, 1763–1814:

I was born on an insignificant island of the West Indies. I was twice married. My first husband perished by the guillotine during the horrors of the French Revolution, and only the death of Robespierre saved me from sharing his fate. When I wedded a second time people thought the man to whom I gave my heart was beneath me in rank; but he made himself the head of the army, and then the ruler of the nation. He it was who said to me, " I win battles but you win hearts." As long as he was true to me he gained triumph after triumph, but when, for selfish reasons, he set me aside and married another, his star began to decline, and he died a prisoner and in exile. I did not long survive him; all the people mourned for me, for they called me "the guardian angel of France."

All the others:

> " With reason firm, and temperate will,
>> Endurance, foresight, strength, and skill,—
>> A perfect woman, nobly planned
>> To warn, to comfort, and command."
>>> —*Adapted from Wordsworth.*

Lucretia Mott, 1793–18—:

On a little island on the bleak coast of New England my childhood's days were passed. At fifteen years of age I began to teach school; at eighteen I was married; at twenty-five I became a minister in the Society of Friends. In addition to what I said in meeting, I spoke often and earnestly in behalf of peace, woman's rights, and the abolition of slavery. I was often in the midst of mobs and violence, but no one ever did me harm, and I lived to see the chains fall from every slave in my native land. But although engaged in so many public duties, I never forgot that a woman's first thought should be for her home and her family; and now, when I am no longer in their midst, children and children's children hold my memory dear.

All the others :

> " Blessing she was; God made her so,
>> And deeds of week-day holiness
>> Fell from her, noiseless as the snow,
>> Nor did she ever chance to know
>> That aught were easier than to bless."
>>> —*Adapted from Lowell.*

Elizabeth Barrett Browning, 1807–1861 :

England was the country of my birth, Italy the land of my adoption. The laurels that adorn my brow were won, not by the sword, but by the pen. I did not lead armies to battle, like Joan of Arc, but I inspired soldiers by my poems; I did not plead the cause of woman from the platform, as did Lucretia Mott, but, like her, I showed mankind what a woman can do; I was not sovereign of a nation, like Elizabeth, but my empire is greater than hers, for the world has crowned me Queen of Poetry.

All the others:

> " She sang the song of Italy ;
> She wrote Aurora Leigh."

Harriet Beecher Stowe, 1812 :

I was born in New England, and, like a true New England girl, I began early in life to grapple with deep theological subjects; before I was twelve years old I wrote an essay upon the question, " Can the immortality of the soul be proved by the light of nature ?" When I became a woman I wrote novels instead of theology ; the greatest of these stirred the pulse of the nation, and helped to break the bondman's chain; it has been translated into every European language, and has been read and re-read by the people of my native land.

> " When truth herself was slavery's slave,
> My hand the prisoned suppliant gave
> The rainbow wings of fiction."

All the others :

" When a deed is done for freedom, through the broad
   earth's aching breast,
Runs a thrill of joy prophetic, trembling on from east to
   west."—*Lowell.*

Grace Darling, 1815–1842 :

My home was on a rocky island on the north-eastern coast of England. My father was a light-house keeper. My life on earth was less than half of the allotted three score years and ten, but I lived long enough to save nine other lives. One night a ship was wrecked upon our coast, and in the morning we saw some people clinging to the distant rocks. I persuaded my father to help me row a boat over the angry waters. We reached them, and brought them all safe to the shore.

All the others:

> " The shortest life is longest if 'tis best,—
> 'Tis ours to work, to God belongs the rest;
> Our lives are measured by the deeds we do,
> The thoughts we think, the objects we pursue."

Florence Nightingale, 1820 :

1 am an English woman, but I was born in a sunny Italian city, whose beautiful name became my own. I, too, saved many lives, but my work was on the field of battle, and not on the stormy ocean. The soldiers in the hospitals were wounded and dying,—many of them dying from inattention and neglect. I went among them, ministered to their wants, dressed their wounds, and spoke words of cheer; and some of them loved me so well, that they even kissed my shadow, as it fell upon the wall.

All the others:

> " On England's annals, through the long
> Hereafter of her speech and song,
> The lady with a lamp shall stand
> In the great history of the land,
> A noble type of good,
> Heroic womanhood."—*Longfellow.*

Jenny Lind, 1821 :

I was born in the Northland, but I have made the world my country, for I charmed both hemispheres by my song. Those who heard me count the time thus spent among the

golden hours of their lives. And now, when the young
men rave about Nilsson, and Gerster, and Patti, the old
men shake their heads and say, " Yes, their voices are
wonderful, but you should have heard the Swedish Nightingale !"

All the others :

"Sound of vernal showers
      On the twinkling grass,
    Rain-awakened flowers,
      All that ever was
Joyous or sweet or clear thy music did surpass."
                                        —*Shelley.*

Harriet Hosmer, 1831 :

I came from the old Bay State, whence have sprung so
many famous men and women. In my childhood's days
I lived out of doors ; I learned to ride, row, swim, and
shoot ; I spent many an hour modeling figures in clay.
When I became a woman I studied art, and now I work
in marble. I have wandered from my native land, and
my home is in Italy, the land of artists. But many of
my creations have found their way to my own country,
and America is proud of the woman, who, as a sculptor
stands first among her sisters.

All the others :

"Maiden, when such a soul as thine is born,
    The morning stars their ancient music make,
    And, joyful, once again their song awake."
                                        —*Lowell.*

All :

The lesson of our lives is this,—
    That woman's sphere is wide ;
  That what by women has been **done,**
    By women may be tried.

You may not win a noble name,
  Such honor falls to few;
Whatever work lies next your hand,
  That work God means for you.

Then do it wisely, do it well;
  Be brave and pure and good;
And, great or small your part in life,
  Hold fast your womanhood.
      [FINIS.]

ELIZABETH LLOYD.

GENEVRA.

Founded on the legend as told in the old song entitled, "The Mistletoe Bough."

CHARACTERS.

LOVELL—the bridegroom.
GENEVRA—the bride.
A KNIGHT.
A LADY.
Guests as many as desirable.
A bevy of lads and lassies for last scene.

SCENE I.

After the wedding—Genevra and guests still in wedding costumes appropriate to the times—Holly, or other evergreen decorations. Antique furnishings for room, stags' horns upon wall, and punch bowl upon the table.

Lovell.—Now, merry hearts, let games begin,
      At games the dullest one may win;
      The prize I've won, bowing full low,
      I own with humble heart doth show
      That daring, not desert, hath won!

Genevra.—The game! the game!
        Lovell, have done.

Knight.—

        Good sir, thy prowess, questioned **never,**
        By us shall be remembered ever,
        If daring wins the fair
        We all will dare [*turning to ladies*]—**beware!**
        But now a game, as says thy bride,
        Now, who?——

Genevra (*exclaims gayly*).—

        I'll hide! I'll hide! I'll hide!
        Lovell, thou'st sought in glen and glade
        The covert where the deer hath stayed ;
        Think'st thou as true thou'lt follow **where**
        I shelter find ? Come, ladies fair,
        Comfort my lord a moment's space.

Lady (*aside*).—

        Genevra, but a moment's grace ;
        I tell thee that his cheek did **pale**
        Its color when beneath thy veil
        A moment you were still as death.
        I watched him then—his fitful breath
        Came in short gasps—he loves thee **well ;**
        Stay not too long in covert dim
        Out of sweet pity unto him!

Genevra.—Fie! fie my own!

        Hast heard it said ?—
        I have !— When once a man is **wed**
        Tease and elude and still mock on,
        If wife will keep what maid hath **won!**
        I'll find a nook—a half-hour's rest
        From eager groom and tiresome **guest !**

[Turns to company.]

Turn to the wall each happy face!
Each hide the eyes a little space!
Count one, two, three, and so to **ten;**
From ten go on to ten again.
And now I go! Who findeth me
May claim my hand for dances **three,**
May drink my health, be first to **call**
Me hostess true of Lovell Hall!

Guests in concert (to music if wished).—
            One, two, three, four, five six, seven, **eight,**
                    nine, ten !

Lovell.—Now, friends, we'll count it once **again.**

Guests (in concert).—
            And one, two, three, and—

Lovell.—Seven are ten ! [*Laughter.*]

Knight.—Away ! away ! I heard her feet
            Fly soft but fleet—yes, soft and **fleet—**
            Past me. This doorway I will **try**

A guest.—
            And this one I !

Another guest.—And this one I !

(All go out by different exits—remain a little time—music.)

SCENE II.
All re-enter, some laughing and breathless, Lovell half anxious

Lady.—We searched the gallery long and dim,
            Afraid each pictured, armored knight
            Might leap from arras, niche, or wall,
            Till we were half aswooned from **fright !**
            She did not answer to **our call.**

4 *Gentleman.*—

I half had sworn I heard her sigh,
As she were frighted too, when I
Looked back of moth-worn velvet chairs,
Where saints above once knelt at prayers—
I list'n'd again.

In the old wall
I heard the wainscot-mouse; an' the fall
And sough o' the wind "in turret and tree,"
Sounded so long and dismally
That had my lady fair been hid
In that ghostly chamber, even she—
A bride—had hailed me rapturously!

Lovell (to first lady).—

My lady fair, what said she when
She smiled and whispered unto thee?

And then
Challenged us to this search?

Lady.—   That she
Would find a half-hour's rest! [*teasingly*]
Be free from her dear lord and tiresome guest!

Lovell (ponders—then speaks).—

Go on with mirth and laugh and jest,
I, only will prolong the quest,
I' faith I swear I think 'twere best
Her lord claim guerdon and not guest!

(*Lovell goes out—music and the minuet, or games, or a song, as performers choose—occasionally one looks anxiously or another listens for Lovell's return.*)

(*Enter Lovell.*)

Lovell.—Is she not here?
              A little fear
              Unmans a man!
(Sinks down half smiling.   They gather about him.)

First Lady.—

              Have courage! More she said:
              'Twere well and good
              A husband, like a lover, should
              Know worth of her so surely won
              By arts such as his heart had won!
              Mayhap about her bridal gear
              She's thrown some cloak, and no doubt
              Where shadows lurk she's crouched in rest,
              In sleep forgetting lord and guest!
              Again we'll search, and revelrie
              Led by her on shall be less dree!

              Come one, come all, if Lovell then,
              Unlike most lords, must find again
              His bride! Away! away! away!

*(They go as gayly as before—presently music of a dirge
sounds faintly—they come in one by one, look blankly at
each other, whisper, shake their heads, try to smile—Lovell
staggers in.)*

Lovell (despairingly).—Is she not here?

                                        O friends of mine!
              Once, heated by the fumes of wine,
              I did a wrong to one! But now
              I did remember how a prayer
              From my foe's lips was sent to heaven!—
              'Twas this—

                  " May joys fall with'ring at his touch,
                  May happiness but mock his gaze"—

Then turning where I stood,
Remorseful, even before my deed
Had been recorded with a .speed
Of word and blow that took my breath,
He hissed, " I'll follow thee like Death,
Ay, will be Death to all thy good!"
My friends, he made a cross in blood,
The blood—my blood his hand had drawn,
Swore by that cross, and swearing fled!
My bride! my bride! alas, is dead!
(*They draw about him to comfort, and curtain falls.*)

SCENE III.

*A garret—chests about—dark corners—young voices heard
approaching—a gay company enter.*

Young Girl.—

Uncle Lovell said we may
Find in these old chests well stored
Some old costumes for our play.

Another.—Dear old man! alway, alway
Striving hard to please us well.
Poor old man! Striving hard to cover
With dear smiles his sadness over,
Lest our hearts be chilled foretime.

Another.—See this old, worm-eaten hold
Of satin, silver, plumes, and gold!
Strong the lock and firm the lid,
Help me, Conrad! [*Looks in as lid is lifted*]
Lo! amid
Dust and darkness, like a star,
Something shines—What is't? A ring!

A diamond circle! Strange sole thing
For such great chest and hasp and key!
                              (*Takes up ring.*)

Another.—Alice! Alice! Let me see!

Conrad.—Alice! All! What can this mean?
            Yes, it must be!
                        This has been
            The silent grave of her so dear,
            So greatly mourned this many a year.

Alice.—Oh! what woe! what woe!
            Strange they never thought to look
            Within, when every crevice, nook,
            And forest even searched they through!
            It cannot be our uncle knew
            This secret spring had e'er been tried
            By his Genevra.
                        Poor young bride!
            How glad and gay and sweet and fair
            She must have been!
                        And oh! that there
            She should have died!
                        It must be so!

Anne.—And the years that he has wandered far and
            wide,
            By plain and sea and mountain side,
            Ever thinking it might be
            He yet would find her—piteously
            Scanning every crowded mart
            With eager eyes and eager heart.
            At last come home to end his life
            In striving thus to make us glad
            In every way—by every plan

He could devise. Dear, sad old man,
How can we tell him what we've found ?
(*Lovell enters, old, gray, and smiling pathetically. He catches
sight of chest and ring, grasps the latter and cries*).—
Oh ! my bride ! my love ! my wife ! my pride !
(*Conflicting emotions depicted on every face*).
This is where she hid, and, prisoned, died !
(*Falls on knees, burying face in hands and leaning on chest.*)
[CURTAIN 'FALLS.]
Music low and mournful, or the singing of "Oh ! the
Mistletoe Bough," by a concealed choir may fittingly fol-
low the fall of the curtain.

EMMA SOPHIE STILWELL.

———— • ————

CONTESTING FOR A PRIZE.

CHARACTERS.

JOHN SEYMOUR, Professor of Elocution.
PAUL RODGERS. Judge.
JULIA GRAY, ⎫
ALICE HILL, ⎬ Contestants.
JENNIE DREW. ⎭

SCENE.—*Parlor, in which Professor S. is seated. Enter
Paul Rodgers.*

Prof. S.—My dear sir, I thank you heartily for the kindness which has prompted you to serve as judge upon this
occasion.

Mr R—Not at all, sir—not at all; the only question in
my mind is why you should have so honored me.

Prof. S.—Whom should one promote to the position of
judge, pray, if not a promising young lawyer.

Mr. R.—Again you honor me [*bowing*].

Prof. S.—Having expressed my appreciation of your

kindness, we will proceed to the business at hand. For some years past it has been my custom at the end of a course of instruction to present a gold medal to the pupil who shall prove most efficient in the art of elocution. During the whole term of the present class three young ladies have stood side by side, their examination proving them of equal merit, therefore a decision must be reached through other means. The method chosen I have already described to you. The trial sentence consists of the two words, "Take this." You are to describe the positions, and the characters to be personated.

Mr. R.—I understand perfectly.

Prof. S.—At the close of the contest you will award the prize to the young lady you consider most deserving.

Mr. R.—Exactly.

Prof. S.—I am expecting the young ladies at half-past ten. [*Glancing at his watch.*] It is already time they were here. [*Voices without, a knock at the door; the Professor rising, opens it; enter three young ladies.*]

Prof. S.—Good-morning, young ladies.

Alice.—Good-morning.

Jennie.—Good-morning, Professor.

Julia.—Good-morning.

Prof. S.—Allow me to present to you your judge, Mr. Paul Rodgers. Mr. Rodgers, let me make you acquainted with the contestants, Miss Julia Gray, Miss Alice Hill, and Miss Jennie Drew.

Mr. R.—Most happy to meet you.

Prof. S.—And now, Mr. Rodgers, we will proceed with the contest.

Jennie (aside).—He doesn't look very severe.

Alice (nervously).—But, Professor Seymour, we have not the least idea upon what we are to contest.

Prof. S.—Mr. Rodgers will explain.

Jennie.—You are not going to be very hard with us, are you, Mr. Rodgers? My memory is most treacherous.

Mr. R.—Your memory will be taxed very little.

Jennie (aside to Alice).—Julia isn't going to waste her vocal powers; she has not said one word since she came in.

Alice.—Oh! she's sure of winning the prize, I can see that plainly.

Mr. R.—Are you ready, young ladies?

Chorus.—Quite ready.

Mr. R.—You are to remember but two words—"Take this." I will picture for you the characters, conditions, and surroundings, and you will express them in those two words.

Jennie.—Or, rather, we will endeavor to do so. [*Withering glance from Julia.*]

Mr. R.—Miss Gray, imagine yourself the queenly daughter of a royal father, surrounded by all the luxury and beauty, art and nature can afford, at your feet the favorite knight of the moment; in your hand the token of that favor, which you present to him with those words.

Julia.—Take this.

Mr. R.—Miss Hill, you are to personate a nursery maid entering a room, which ten minutes ago you left in perfect order, but which has been completely transformed in that short space of time by a small boy. Your patience is tried to such an extent that you smack the offender's hands.

Alice.—Take this!

Mr. R.—Miss Drew, a widow bends o'er the death-bed of her only child. He has refused to take the medicine upon which her last hope depends. With all her woman's heart in her voice she beseeches him.

Jennie.—Take this.

Mr. R.—Professor, I understand we were to have six characters, each young lady representing two.

Prof. S.—That is correct—proceed.

Mr. R.—Once more, Miss Gray, the scene is that of a children's festival. At the moment they are enjoying, as only children can, ice-cream, cakes, and candies. One little maiden has already before her a plate of ice-cream, of which she evidently approves, as she advises her little neighbor in the most audible whisper, to "Take this," pointing to the particular variety on her plate.

Miss Gray.—Take this. [*Every one smiles, Mr. R. uses handkerchief, fearing to show too much enjoyment.*]

Mr. R.—You, Miss Hill, are to imagine a pretty drawing-room, in the middle of which stands a wee baby boy, hesitating, tottering; at a little distance a lady, holding in her hand a bright toy, for which she is endeavoring to persuade the child to take its first steps.

Alice.—Take this.

Mr. R.—Miss Drew, you are to become for the time being, a little country girl, who has had the misfortune to offend her lover. He is a young man from the city, who, having won her heart among other summer pastimes, refuses now to have his wrath appeased, although she offers him the red rose that hides in her sunny hair, the last of the woodland flowers that are pinned to her dress—in fact, any of her treasures, until in desperation she bashfully offers him a kiss.

Jennie (*bashfully twisting her dress, hesitating, sidling closer to the judge*).—Take this.

Mr. R. (*bending over quickly, attempts to kiss her*).

Jennie.—Mr. Rodgers!

Alice.—Oh!

Julia.—How shocking!

Prof. S.—What does this mean, sir?

Mr. R.—I beg your pardon, Miss Drew—Professor Seymour—ladies. You are surely convinced of this fact, that I had no intention of insulting Miss Drew. My explanation for so unaccountable, so unmanly an act is this: Miss Drew was completely lost in the character she personated, and for the moment I saw—knew only the country maiden, and myself became the appeased lover. Weak as the explanation may seem, it is all I have to give, but it is an honest one.

Prof. S.—Had you been a stranger I should doubt your word, as it is, I truly believe you.

Julia (*aside*).—It is all her fault, anyhow. She had no right to look at him in such an insinuating manner.

Alice.—Absurd. She had a right to make it as natural as possible.

Mr. R.—This unfortunate occurrence makes the one deserving of the prize apparent to you all. To lead the audience to forget the speaker and know only the character portrayed is the aim of every true artist; but, in addition to this, to make the judge forget he is a judge, is certainly the crowning achievement.

Miss Drew, pardon me, and allow me the honor of presenting you with this medal, of which you are so worthy.

(*Miss Drew, accepting the medal, bows.*)

[FINIS.]

ADELINE B. AVERY.

THE SPIRIT OF LIBERTY.

CHARACTERS.

MARTHA.
MARIAN EUTASIA.
OTHER LADIES.

SCENE I.

Martha, a young lady, attired in the fashion of 1776, seated in a humble room at a spinning-wheel, which she works at intervals, while she recites the following stanzas, the refrain being recited (or sung) by a concealed chorus of young ladies.

Martha.—Bright is the moon that hangs aloft;
  The air of night is sweet and soft;
  The stars, that ne'er a tear have shed,
  Are full of gold smiles overhead.
Chorus.—Little they know of Boston tea,
  Or the great price of liberty.

Martha.—The forest paths, all broad and free,
  That stretch their arms invitingly,
  Are edged with moss, begemmed with flowers,
  They know no sad, no anxious hours.
Chorus.—No breaking hearts, no Boston tea,
  Or the sad price of liberty.

Martha.—The fringed grass the clover holds,
  Each day accustomed beauty molds.
  Nature, in her most perfect plan,
  Seems mocked alone by struggling man.
Chorus.—He spilled, alas, the Boston tea,
  And vowed the vow of liberty.

(She ceases singing and spins a few moments steadily, then the wheel moves slowly and she sings)—

Martha.—Strong and firm is the thread I spin,
            To wrap the forms I love within.
            Heavy of texture, it shall keep
            My soldiers warm, when cold winds sweep.
    Chorus.—Sweep o'er them, as for Boston tea
            They strike the blow of liberty.

Martha.—Could I but turn my flax to brass
            Through which no sword or shot could pass;
            A buckler spin impregnable,
            That would each British ball repel,
    Chorus.—Then could we smile at Boston tea,
            Nor dread the price of liberty.

Martha.—Still, grief for labor must make way,
            And hands not rest that voice have sway,
            For independence was declared—
            We'll have it while an arm is spared!
    Chorus.—Nor pay a tax on Boston tea.
            We'll work and fight for liberty!

(She spins rapidly a little while, then ceases, saying plaintively.)

Martha.—At Lexington my father fell,
            And brothers two. Who can foretell
            What will befall the younger boys,
            And he who was to share my joys?
    Chorus.—The price, the price of Boston tea,
            The heavy price of liberty.

(She turns the wheel a few rounds slowly, then sings cheer fully.)

Martha.—If they can fight with dauntless heart,
          Shall we not try to do our part?
          So that at last the right may win,
          We'll pray for courage while we spin.
    Chorus.—The hearts that sank the Boston tea
          Will, conquering, gain sweet liberty.

Martha.—This spinning-wheel must swiftly turn
          Until the sun of morning burn.
          These robes are needed. I must break
          This spell of thought, and silence take—
    Chorus.—With labor, for the Boston tea
          Sank, and up rose our liberty.

          (She spins on swiftly and steadily.)
              [CURTAIN FALLS.]

              SCENE II., 1876.

An elegantly furnished apartment. Marian Eutasia, a fashionable young lady of the present day, seated in an easy chair. She yawns, then recites (or sings) in tone to suit the words. The chorus gives the refrain in a spirit of mockery or ridicule.

Eutasia.—I wonder what I'll do
          This dreary evening through?
          No theatre or ball,
          No company, large or small,
          Invites me to go out.
          The novels are all done,
          I've read them every one;

They're full of prosy stuff,
With not half love enough
To compass them about.
Chorus.—She hasn't love enough,
    But only prosy stuff.

Eutasia.—I might some thought inclose
In petals of a rose,
Or weave into a seam
The mystery of some dream,
My handiwork to show;
But where would be the use?
Genius is so prófuse
With all his lavish gifts,
Fame lodges but in drifts
On those he best doth know.
Chorus.—Fame lodges but in drifts
    With all his lavish gifts.

Eutasia.—I wish I'd lived before!
A hundred years or more.
Talents were rare and pure,
And critics more demure.
I might have shone a star.
People could labor then,
But seldom drive a pen;
Could work and be content
Until their lives were spent,
Nor think of journeying far.
Chorus.—We wish she'd lived before
    A hundred years or more.

Eutasia.—This is a restless age,
    Each year a crowded page:

The people run to brains
And groan with aches and pains.
'Tis sad it must be so.
I long that I may see
Within this century
Some vision of the past,
Some form of ancient cast
To cheer me as I go.

Chorus.—The people run to brains
         And groan with aches and pains.

(She ceases, leans back in her luxurious arm-chair, and sleeps. Enter Martha in the garb we saw her last, attended by several elegantly attired young ladies of the present day, who constituted the concealed chorus. The ladies assist Martha noiselessly to an elevated seat and kneel at her feet reciting or singing)—

Queen, we are worshipers
At thy fair shrine.

(Marian wakes and gazes curiously at the tableaux.)

Queen, we are worshipers
Whilst thou recline.

We of this century
Give reverence due,
We of this century
Our praise renew.

(Marian rises and kneels with the others, joining in the song.)

Queen, we are worshipers
At thy fair shrine.
Queen, we are worshipers
Whilst thou recline.

Thank thee that liberty
Came to us free!
Thank thee for liberty,
Our legacy!

Queen, we are worshipers
At thy fair shrine.
Queen, we are worshipers
Whilst thou recline.

We of this century
Give reverence due.
We of this century
Our praise renew.

[CURTAIN FALLS.]

MRS. S. L. OBERHOLTZER.

TRAPPED.

A COMEDY IN ONE ACT.

CHARACTERS.

DICK ROY, aged twenty-one years.
JANET ROY, his sister, aged twenty-three years.
NELLIE TAYLOR, his sweetheart, aged twenty years.
SARAH, a servant.

SCENE.—*A cozy little breakfast room. Table in centre set for breakfast; desk or table at right, lounge or sofa at left. Entrances right and left. Window at back covered by a curtain. Dick Roy discovered seated at desk with papers before him. Holds up letter he has just finished writing and looks at it critically. Then in pantomime compares it with another folded letter which he takes up from the desk.*

Dick.—A nice way to begin a man's career, I'm sure. Forgery. Well, well, it's in a good cause and nobody's name has been forged but my sister's, and I am sure she won't mind. [*Leaning over and putting a mark on one of the letters.*] Ah! that robs my act of its criminal character. Beneath Janet's name I put my own initial, so small that nobody would ever notice it, to be sure, but the loop of the R is big enough for one to crawl through. [*Rings bell for servant and then puts letter in addressed envelope.*]

(*Enter Sarah, L.*)

Dick.—Sarah, I wish you would have this letter delivered by messenger immediately. It is for Miss Taylor, you see, and she only lives a few blocks away.

Sarah.—All right, sir. Will you have your breakfast now, sir, or wait for Miss Janet?

Dick.—I'll wait. Sarah.

Sarah.—As you please, sir. And here's that you may have many more birthdays, sir.

Dick.—Thank you, Sarah; thank you. And you'll never be afraid of burglars or ghosts any more now, will you, since there's a man in the house?

Sarah (*laughing*).—Never again, sir. But you don't look a bit more of a man than you did yesterday, sir.

Dick.—But I am, Sarah—I am, you know. I'm twenty-one to-day, and a man and a voter.

Sarah.—So you are, sir. [*Exit, L.*]

Dick.—And a lover, I might have added, for there's no mistaking I'm in love with that little witch, Nellie Taylor, bless her! Though for the life of me I can't tell whether she cares a whit more for me than she does for the other fellows she smiles on, and she smiles on them all with an impartiality that is simply exasperating. Jolly girl! I suppose she hasn't heard I've been home with a cold for the last week or she'd have been around here. I may flatter myself, but I think she would.

(*Enter Janet Roy, L.*)

Janet.—Good-morning, Dick. Many happy returns.

Dick.—Good-morning, Jean, and thank you. If I were a girl I'd make a curtsy, but I'm a man and can't—and a hungry man, too, feeling much better than for a week past, and ready to wrestle with a good, substantial breakfast.

Janet (*sitting down at the table*).—For all of which I am more than thankful, my dear brother. Come, let us see if we can't diminish that appetite somewhat. [*Ringing bell.*]

Dick.—With all my heart. [*Joining Janet at the table. Enter Sarah, L., with breakfast, coffee-urn, etc., which she places on the table, and then takes two letters from her pocket, which she hands to Janet and goes out, L.*]

Janet (*after glancing at the superscription*).—Here is a letter for you, sir, if your name be Horatio! [*Reaching letter across table to Dick.*]

Dick.—But my name is not Horatio. [*Taking it.*] Are you aware that to paraphrase is perfectly allowable? "If your name be Richard" would be much more appropriate and would sound far better. Look, for instance, at the Third Witch—glorious example for all paraphrasers—who, on hearing a trumpet sound when the lines call for a drum, had the presence of mind to exclaim: "A trumpet! a trumpet! Macbeth doth stump it!"

(*Janet meanwhile has torn open her letter, which is black-bordered, and has drawn out the inclosure with considerable agitation. She reads it through and her face assumes a saddened expression.*)

Dick.—What's the matter?

Janet.—Uncle Arthur is dead.

Dick.—Uncle Arthur! Uncle Arthur! Let's see. Uncle

Arthur is one of my respected great-uncles, whom I have never had the pleasure of seeing—a California million-aire. I wonder did it ever strike him that a little of his wealth would be acceptable to his great-niece and great-nephew, who are battling with the world far away over here in the East.

Janet.—O Dick! How can you talk of the poor man's money when he is just dead?

Dick (laughing.)—Poor man! I always thought he was a rich one.

Janet.—I suppose he was, but then you need have no thought of any legacy. I expect he has left everything to his daughter, Margaret, and her son, Harry.

Dick.—Oh, of course there is no such good luck for me as getting money that I haven't worked for. [*Meanwhile he has opened his own letter, which he now proceeds to read.*]

Janet.—May I inquire what Nell has to say this morning?

Dick (after a pause).—How do you know it is from Nell?

Janet.—I know her handwriting.

Dick.—But it's just like hundreds of others. [*Putting the letter in his pocket.*] All ladies write in the same style nowadays. The letters are all very tall and all very thin.

Janet.—Each lady's hand has a peculiarity, neverthe-less.

Dick.—Which nobody can deny! Some hands are pink and some are white, some are fat and some are lean, some wear diamonds and some wear none.

Janet.—How you trip one up! You know very well what I mean. Would you have me stumble over the whole length of chirography every time?

Dick.—By no means. It would only be a waste of breath.

Janet.—By the bye, speaking of some hands with diamonds and some without, Nell doesn't wear one, does she? When do you propose presenting her with one of those gems.

Dick.—I was not aware that young men are generally expected to provide their lady friends with diamond rings.

Janet.—Did the fact that there is such a thing as an engagement ring ever dawn upon your enlightened intellect?

Dick.—Engagement! Did I understand you to say engagement? Since when, pray, did you conclude that your respected brother had given his heart to another? I know of no engagement.

Janet.—Oh! dear. Have I really been mistaken? And here I was already congratulating myself on so soon having a sister-in-law!

Dick.—Do you remember the old rhyme:

"Can the love that you're so rich in
    Build a fire in the kitchen?
    Or the little god of love turn the spit, spit, spit?"

I should hesitate, I think, to ask any one to marry me for fear of having that couplet thrown in my face. Now, if that dear old great-uncle of ours had only taken it into his aged head to leave us a few of his many thousands, then perhaps I might think of engagements and diamond rings and mothers-in-law, and you might begin to speculate on the comparative advantages of my various lady friends as sisters-in-law.

Janet.—Poor, dear old man! I can just remember sitting on his knee and playing with his long beard at the time he was on from the West. It's really a shame, Dick, our being so lively, and Uncle Arthur, grandfather's own brother, lying dead.

Dick.—Well, my dear, I should be lying alive if I said I was sorry he's gone; for while there's death there's hope, and who knows but he may have thought of us? You know, Jean, I never saw the old gentleman, and it's not to be expected I shall be awfully cut up over his shuffling off this mortal coil; but, I say, if you really feel sad about it, you'd better go down town immediately and buy a black alpaca dress and a long crape veil.

Janet.—O Dick!

(*Enter Sarah with yellow envelope in her hand, L.*)

Sarah.—I hope you'll excuse me, Mr. Dick, but I find I entirely forgot to give you this letter, which I just discovered in my pocket. It came in the morning mail, sir.

Dick (*taking the letter*).—All right, Sarah. Let's see what it is. [*Exit Sarah, L. Dick tears open envelope and extracts letter. As he reads his face brightens.*] Hurrah! Hurrah for Uncle Arthur! Hurrah, Jean, we've been left a fortune!

Janet (*disbelieving*).—If you must joke, Dick, pray don't take such a subject.

Dick.—But I'm not joking; it's a fact. Here is a letter from the dear old man's lawyer. Look at the postmark; look at the letter-head; read the message. [*He goes around to her and spreads the letter before her.*] There, read. [*Reads.*]

"RICHARD ROY, ESQ.: DEAR SIR:—I have pleasure in informing you that the will of the late Arthur Roy, Esq., of this city, bequeaths to his great-nephew and great-niece, Richard and Janet Roy (yourself and sister), each the sum of fifty thousand dollars. These amounts are invested in United States Government bonds and shall be forwarded to you in due course.

"I have the honor to be your obedient servant,

"J. MADISON PERRY, Executor."

Janet.—Poor Uncle Arthur! [*Then she breaks into sobs and buries her face in her handkerchief, weeping.*]

Dick (*smoothing her hair*).—What is the matter with you? I can't see anything to cry about. You seem rather mixed on the question of the time to laugh and the time to weep.

Janet (*between her sobs*).—O Dick! I believe you have no feeling at all. Just to think what a dear, kind uncle we have lost. How good of him to remember us!

Dick.—Very good of him indeed, sister mine, but I can't see that that ought to make one sad. Rather a cause for rejoicing, I should say. Poor fellow he was so old he couldn't enjoy life, and I dare say he's better off where he is—that is, if he was as good as his will makes me think he was. But never mind, dear, go to your room and have your cry out.

Janet (*rising and going out*).—O Dick! If you love me, please don't joke about it, for I really do feel terribly. [*Exit, R.*]

Dick (*resuming his seat at the desk*).—Poor girl, she is rather cut up, but I am sure I'm not. I may naturally be light-hearted, and to leave me fifty thousand dollars is not exactly the way to make me melancholy and sad. [*A ring is heard, as of a door bell.*] Ah! ten to one that's Nell. Now, Dicky, old boy, hide yourself and prepare for action. [*Gets behind curtain of window at back. Sarah goes through, entering one door, L., and going out of the other, R.*]

Dick (*poking his head from between curtains.*)—In three

minutes I shall know whether Nell Taylor loves me or not, provided my little scheme don't miscarry, of which I have hopes it won't.

(*Enter Sarah, R., followed by Nellie Taylor, who shows signs of weeping and now and then wipes her eyes.*)

Nellie.—Please tell Miss Janet I would like to see her.

Sarah.—Yes, miss; and you'll excuse the breakfast table, miss, won't you? I haven't had time to clear the things away, as you see.

Nellie.—O! certainly, Sarah; certainly. [*Exit Sarah, R. Nellie sits on lounge.*]

Nellie (*solil.*).—And there was where poor, dear Dick used to eat [*looking at table*]. How on earth could Janet swallow a mouthful this morning, I wonder? I'm sure I could not. The sad news took my appetite every bit away. And there are two places. I suppose his aunt or somebody is here.

(*Enter Janet, R., with red eyes and like Nellie, using handkerchief. Nellie rises and goes to her.*)

Nellie.—O Jean! I do so sympathize with you. [*Dick looks out from curtains and grins.*] Come and sit down by me. Trouble comes to all of us some time, you know. [*Both go to sofa and sit down.*]

Janet.—But, my dear Nell—

Nellie.—There, now, don't speak to me of it. Don't tell me how much worse you feel than I. I know you think so; but, indeed [*weeping*], you do not know how I loved him!

(*Dick makes grimaces of delight from curtain.*)

Janet (*aside*).—Perhaps Uncle Arthur was related to the Taylors. [*Aloud*]. Was he—

Nellie.—Didn't you know it? Oh! why didn't some one let me know that he was so ill? I would have so liked to be with him.

Dick (from curtain).—Jean must think she was very fond of Uncle Arthur. Ha, ha! Grim sort of a joke, ain't it?

Janet.—Was he so very dear to you?

Nellie.—O Jean! you cannot imagine how we loved each other. There was no time set, but then it was understood that it was to come off as soon as his salary was sufficient for him to—

Janet.—What do you mean? What was to come off?

Nellie.—We were engaged, you know.

Janet (surprised).—Engaged!

Nellie.—Did you not know it?

Janet.—Nell, what are you talking about?

Nellie.—Are you angry? Would you not have approved of his making me his wife?

Janet.—You marry Uncle Arthur!

Nettie (in surprise).—Uncle Arthur! Who is Uncle Arthur?

Janet.—The dear, kind old gentleman who has just died.

Nellie.—But I have been talking of Dick. You must have known I was. Poor, dear Dick! [*Falls to weeping again.*]

Janet.—But Dick is not dead.

Nellie (rising to her feet in glad surprise).—Not dead?

Dick (coming from behind the curtain).—No, you darling, good girl; now I believe you do care a little bit for me.

Janet.—But I cannot understand it. Whatever could have caused you to think Dick was dead?

Nellie.—The idea of asking me after the letter you wrote. Didn't you tell me so? I didn't think, Jean, that you could perpetrate such an awful joke.

Janet.—But I wrote no letter.

(*Nellie draws a letter from her pocket and hands it to Janet.*)

Nellie.—Read it.

Janet (reading).—   "FRIDAY MORNING.

"MY DEAR NELL.—I have sad news for you. Our darling boy is no more. At twelve o'clock last night he breathed his last. Oh, how can I write it? I can scarcely realize that he is gone. Please do come around and see me. I know you thought a great deal of him and can sympathize with me.   "Ever yours,

                          "JANET ROY."

[*Speaking*].—But it is not my writing. I never make my e's that way, nor sign myself "ever yours."

Nellie.—It is very like your writing, and I saw the windows bowed. Who could have written it if you didn't?

Dick (with some pride).—I am the author. It was a little trap, and it worked admirably—far better than I expected.

Nellie and Janet (in chorus).—You awful boy!

Dick.—The boy is dead!

Nellie.—But what a frightful story you told, and how terribly I was worried!

Dick.—It is all true. There is not an untruth in the whole letter. The boy is no more; the boy did breathe his last. I am a man now. This is my twenty-first birthday.

Janet.—But you forged my name.

Dick.—But I put my initial below it [*pointing to the place*], as you will notice. And [*turning to Nell*] our wedding will be just as soon as you can get ready. The interest of fifty thousand dollars, which you must know the puzzling Uncle Arthur just left me, plus my salary, is all sufficient, isn't it? And I say, Jean, how do you like the prospect of a sister-in-law? I trapped her, didn't I?

Nellie.—And she was glad to be trapped.

                [CURTAIN.]

THE RAILWAY MATINEE.

ARRANGED BY MARGUERITE W. MORTON.

CHARACTERS.

MISS PRECISION.	ROARER.
FOGG, a deaf old gentleman.	HESITATION.
BRAKEMAN.	

SCENE.—*Interior of a railway car. Several passengers seated. As the curtain rises, the sound of the whistle and the noise of the train just starting are heard. Enter Roarer at back of car. The other passengers, with the exception of Fogg, turn to look at him. He nods pleasantly to all and seats himself opposite Hesitation.*

Fogg (disturbed by the commotion and thinking himself addressed).—Hey? [*All start nervously and speak together.*]

Roarer.—I wa'n't a sayin' nauthin'.

Hesitation.—I-I-I d-d-d-dud-dud-didn't s-s-say n-n-nuth nuthing.

Miss Precision.—I said nothing, sir. [*With great dignity.*]

Other Passengers.—I didn't say nothing.

Fogg (addressing Hesitation, defiantly).—Wha' say?

Hesitation.—I-I-I-I w-w-w-wuh-wuh-wasn'-wasn'—I wasn' s-s-sp-speak—

Fogg.—Hey? [*Louder.*]

Roarer.—He wa'n't sayin' nauthin'! He aint opened his mouth.

Fogg.—Soap in the South? Wha' for?

Miss Precision (very distinctly).—Mouth! Mouth! He said "opened his mouth." The gentleman seated directly opposite you was—

Fogg.—Offers to chew what?

Miss Precision.—Sir, I made no reference whatever to chewing. You certainly misunderstood me.

Hesitation.—I-I-I-I d-d-d-dud-d-d-dud-dud-don't ch-ch-ch—

Fogg.—Hey? [*Very loud.*]

Roarer.—He don't chew nauthin'. He wa'n't a talkin' when you shot off at him.

Fogg.—Who got off? Wha' d' he get off for?

Miss Precision.—You don't appear to comprehend clearly what he stated. No person has left the train.

Fogg.—Then wha' d' he say so for?

Hesitation.—Oh, he d-d-dud-dud-did-did—

Fogg.—Who did?

Hesitation.—Num-num-num-num-n-no-noboby! He-he-he dud-did-d-d-d-didn't—didn't s-s—

Fogg.—Then wha' made you say he did?

Miss Precision.—You misunderstood him. He was probably about to remark that no reference whatever had been intentionally made to the departure of any person from the train, when you interrupted him in the midst of an unfinished sentence, and hence obtained an erroneous impression of the tenor of his remarks. He meant no offense—

Fogg.—Know a fence? Of course I know a fence! Know a fence? Wha' d' you take me for?

Roarer.—He ain't got middlin' good hearin'. Y'ears kind o' stuffed up!

Fogg.—Time to brush up? Wha' for?

Miss Precision.—No! no! He remarked to the other gentleman that your hearing appeared to be rather defective.

Fogg.—His father a detective? Huh!

Hesitation.—N-n-n-n-nun-nun-nun-no! H-h-h-h-he s-s-said you w-w-w-wuh-was a little d-d-d-dud-dud-deaf!

Fogg (*springing to his feet*).—Said I was a thief! Said I was a thief! Wha' d'ye mean? Show him to me! Who says I am a thief? Who says so?

Roarer.—Nobody don't say you ain't no thief. I just said as how we didn't get along very well. You see he [*pointing to Hesitation*] can't talk very well, an'—

Hesitation.—Wh-wh-wh-why c-c-can-can't I t-t-t-tut-tut-tut-talk? I-I-I-I'd like t-to know wh-wh-wh-what's the reason I c-c-can-can't t-t-t-tut-tut-talk as w-w-well as any bub-bub-body that's bub-bub-been tut-tut-talking on this c-c-car ever s-s-since the t-t-tut-tut-train—

Fogg (*suspiciously*).—Hey?

Roarer.—I was sayin' as how he didn't talk middlin' well, an'—

Fogg.—Should say so! [*Seating himself.*]

Roarer.—And you know you can't hear only tollable—

Fogg.—Can't hear! Can't hear! Like to know why I can't hear! Why can't I? Can't hear! If I couldn't hear better than half the people on this train, I'd cut off my ears. Can't hear? It's news to me if I can't! I'd like to know who—

Brakeman (*at door*).—Burlington! Change cars for Keokuk, Ceed Rap's, an' For' Mad'son! This car f'r Omaha? Twen' minuts f'r supper!

(*Several passengers grasp their valises, etc., and prepare to leave the car. Fogg and Hesitation shake their fists at Roarer and talk together.*)

Fogg.—Can't hear! Can't hear! Like to know why I can't hear.

Hesitation.—C-c-can-can't t-t-t-tut-tut-talk! Wh-wh-wh why c-c-can-can't I t-t-t-t-tut-tut-tut-talk?

[QUICK CURTAIN.]

R. J. BURDETTE.

A CHANGED HOUSEWIFE.

CHARACTERS.

JERUSHA, a tidy housewife.   LEO, } her sons.
JEREMIAH, her husband.   FLING, }
MISS PHILANTHROPY, a book agent.

SCENE I.

An ordinary country sitting-room.

Jerusha (sweeping and moving the furniture that her work be thoroughly done).—There's no use trying to keep anything in order in this house with three careless creatures running in and out all the time. It's enough to set a decent woman crazy to see the hats and coats flung around and have no end to the mud dragged in. It's all Jeremiah's fault! If his mother had only brought him up differently! Oh! dear. [*She leans on her broom, then sweeps away vigorously.*]

(*Enter Jeremiah.*)

Jeremiah.—Whew! You must have the lungs of an ox!

Jerusha.—Well, I haint got the strength of one, I'd let you know! and I'm about tired of cleaning after you and your boys!

Jeremiah (aside).—Seems to be a little riled. [*Aloud.*] Take it cool, Jerusha. Everything is made of dust, and us to boot.

Jerusha (holding the door open with her broom).—Take it cool yourself! and clean your boots before you come into this room again.

Jeremiah.—Can't you leave the floors alone, and not be forever stirring up the dirt?

Jerusha (sharply).—No, I can't! You'll not wade knee-deep while I'm your wife, if you are so fond of it.

Jeremiah (half aside).—I may's well go somewhere till the dust settles.

Jerusha.—Do, for pity's sake, go somewhere and stay till dinner time! [*Exit Jeremiah.*]

(*Enter Leo hurriedly, holding a cut finger of one hand tightly in the palm of the other.*)

Leo.—Get me a rag—quick, mother!

Jerusha.—You good-for-nothing, careless creature, to cut yourself. There! Look at your feet—all over mud. You're enough to provoke a saint! I may slave and clean from morning till night, and this is the thanks I get.

Leo.—Won't you tie up my finger, mother? It bleeds so.

Jerusha.—Yes, I s'pose so. For pity's sake don't let the blood drop on the floor. Run out-doors, and I'll bring a rag. [*Exit Leo.*]

Jerusha.—There's no getting to do anything in peace! [*Snatches up a bit of muslin from some convenient place and goes out.*]

(*Enter Fling, from the other side, whistling "Get out of the Wilderness" and dancing a jig to it.*)

Jerusha (calling).—Get out of there, Fling, and stop that noise!

(*Fling whistles and dances more softly.*)

Jerusha (entering).—Where's the use of any living woman having such a worthless boy? Didn't you hear—I said, get-out and be still! Here one boy cuts his finger nearly off, and another is fit to tear the house down! There's no use trying to live!

Fling (subsiding).—Where's Leo? Is he hurt?

Jerusha.—Be sure he's hurt, or I wouldn't a said so.

(*Enter Leo, with his finger clothed in a large rag, around which he is wrapping a string with his other hand.*)

Fling (going forward).—Halloa, Leo! How'd you get hurt, old fellow?

Leo.—Cut with the hatchet, making a new latch for the barn door.

Jerusha.—A likely story! Why can't your father make the latches himself? Here, let me tie it [*turning to the finger*], you're too miserably awkward. [*She winds the string tightly.*]

Leo.—Ouch! That hurts.

Jerusha.—There! Don't be a baby! Now, what you're going to do with yourselves till noon I don't know.

Fling.—Can't we have a game of chess, or some fun? I'll run up and get the chessboard. [*Turning to go out.*]

Jerusha.—I'll have no such wicked nonsense in my house and—[*exit Fling. Calling after him.*] Take off your boots if you go up-stairs! [*To Leo.*] I can't stand this life much longer. It's wear and tear and clean till I go down to the grave, and where's the recompense?

Leo.—I reckon you'll have to count Fling and I on that side.

Jerusha.—A couple of disobedient, spoiled boys. A pretty recompense! Fling's enough to set anybody wild, and you're forever getting upset.

(*Enter Fling, with boots off, bearing a set of dominoes.*)

Fling.—Halloa, Leo, here's a set of dominoes! We'll have a game here. You won't care, mother, will you? We'll be awful quiet.

Jerusha.—Awful quiet! Didn't I tell you I'd have none of your carrying on? [*In a louder tone.*] I must clean up my house and keep it decent if you drive me crazy!

Fling (*to Leo*).—Let's go down to Beck's! They ain't so awful decent—or, hold on, how's your finger?

Leo.—Able to travel. [*Exit Leo and Fling.*]

(*Jerusha resumes her work of cleaning. A rap at the door.*)

Jerusha (aloud).—Come in! [*Aside.*] If you must. What a botheration!

(*Enter Miss Philanthropy, bearing a small satchel.*)

Jerusha (wiping the dust from a chair with her apron, presents it).—Have a seat, will you?

Miss P. (accepting).—Thanks! This is a beautiful spring day.

Jerusha.—Perhaps it is. I haint had time to look it up.

Miss P.—The sun would stream in at your window if you raised the curtain.

Jerusha (emphatically).—I don't raise my curtains and let the sun fade my carpets.

Miss P.—Forgive me, I meant no offense. [*Undoing her satchel and taking therefrom a book.*] Here is a little work on Light and Temperance, madam, I am agent for. Will you look at it?

Jerusha.—No, I haint no time to bother with it. Besides, I can't see without my specs. These subscription books is swindles, any way. Jeremiah and the boys has wasted lots of money on 'em.

Miss P.—This is a valuable book, madam. I have sold a thousand copies. Where are your husband and sons?

Jerusha (snappishly).—I don't know where they are! They're mostly down at Beck's saloon when they ain't draggin' in dirt for me.

Miss P. (aside).—The world is a broad mission field. [*Turning over the leaves of the book thoughtfully.*] Let me read you a few verses from this work.

Jerusha (rubbing her furniture with a duster).—Let them be short then! [*Aside.*] I s'pose a body must be civil.

Miss P. (*reading*).—

> For true discernment we require
>   Outward and inward light,
> Sun rays and soul shine, that we know
>   The day of life from night.
> There is no sky, outward or in,
>   But has its flitting clouds;
> There is no air, though soft as down,
>   But some dull mist enshrouds.
>
> Who sees not light, can feel the dark,
>   And darkness grows apace.
> One soul which has a head-light lost
>   O'ershadows a vast space;
> For, groping on its blinded way,
>   'Mid other flickering flames,
> It lends but a benumbing aid,
>   And ne'er the day proclaims!—
>   [*pausing and looking up.*]

Jerusha.—Funeral hymns, eh? Good enough, but I naint no time to learn 'em.

Miss P.—People bury much of value alive. Listen again! [*She turns to another page and reads:*]

> Open your houses! let the light in,
> Let the boys in with their restless din.
> What are your carpets and unscratched chairs?
> What are your cares and delicate wares?
>
> Make your homes joyful, jubilant, gay!
> Labor, comfort, enjoy and play.
> This much do for the temperance cause;
> Women make better our social laws!

Drive not your children out in the cold,
But gather them closely into the fold.
Let home be the freest place of all;
Let scars on your furniture, not on them, fall.

If the dust lie thick, keep their hearts clear,
Let home be the place of holiest cheer!

Jerusha (who at the first mention of houses had ceased her work to listen).—A pretty doctrine to recommend; the banging up of furniture. Thank goodness, my children are almost men, and they haven't left a scar on nothin' outside the woodshed. Now they're never at home only when they sleep and eat.

Miss P.—Pardon me, but you may live to see the time you would prefer them here.

Jerusha.—I'd like to have them well enough now, if they'd be still and cleanly. That saloon, on the whole, is rather a bad place. I've half a notion to read your book.

Miss P.—I am glad to present you with a copy. [*Rising and handing it to Jerusha.*]

Jerusha (accepting).—I don't say as you need give it to me.

Miss P.—But I wish to. I hope you may see differently and with clearer vision.

[CURTAIN FALLS.]

SCENE II.

The same room in brighter keeping. The curtain raised and light streaming in. The appurtenances of labor out of sight. Jerusha, spectacles on, rocking and reading the book.
(Enter Fling.)

Fling.—Halloa, mother! You look as sweet as pie. Dare I come in?

Jerusha.—Certainly, Fling. Where's your father and Leo ?

Fling (looking at his boots, which he attempts to pull off).—Coming. They weren't quite done the game.

Jerusha.—Never mind your boots, son. I have a new book.

Fling (aside).—I wonder how it turned the tables on boots! And the curtain's up. How jolly! [*He throws himself down on the lounge. Aloud.*] It's enough nicer here than down at Beck's, mother! It's full of tobacco smoke and whisky breaths down there. I wish a fellow didn't have to go!

Jerusha.—You needn't go any more, Fling. I'm going to let you have your games here. I want to learn to play.

Fling (jumping up and seizing her hand).—Give us a shake on that. I'll teach you all the tricks of the trade.

(*Enter Leo.*)

Fling.—Halloa, Leo, mother's going to learn to play chess! And what's more, we're going to do it here. [*He commences to whistle " Get out of the Wilderness" and dance a jig.*]

Leo.—Hold up, Fling! This ain't a circus.

Fling (stops).—I forgot. But it's some jolly good place.

(*Enter Jeremiah.*)

Jeremiah.—What's the clamor, boys? Too much luck!

Fling.—We're the winners. Here's mother.

Jeremiah.—Heigh-oh! What's up, Jerusha?

Jerusha.—Nothing particular. I've been reading.

Jeremiah.—Reading! That's a new dodge. Why don't you talk? Look at these fellows with their boots on! And we're late for dinner.

Jerusha.—Dear Jeremiah, I didn't think it was dinner time.

Jeremiah (*aside*).—Dear Jeremiah! What ails **the** woman?

Fling.—We ain't hungry, mother. Been eatin' peanuts. I brought you some shelled and skinned. [*Taking a handful from his pocket.*] They make an awful litter, you know.

Jerusha (*accepting the kernels*).—Thank you, my boy! Dear Jeremiah, is Beck's a temperance saloon?

Jeremiah (*aside*).—Dear Jeremiah again! She must be going to die. [*Aloud.*] No, 'taint a temperance place, Jerusha. Never was, as I know on. What's your book, that's so amazin' interestin' you forget the old tune of cleanliness? [*taking it from her hand*].

Jerusha.—It gives the blind sight.

Jeremiah.—The coming millennium, I reckon, where people crave books instead of food. Read a chapter, Leo, that we may judge. [*Leo takes the book, opens it, and reads:*]

> Men, who are arbiters of fate,
> Control fate by your will!
> Make it your slave; be masters strong!
> Train it to step and drill.
>
> Be pure, be temperate, true and just,
> Loving and tender, too;
> Then will you ne'er complain of fate
> Or it be false to you.
>
> The lights of earth are fame and power
> Flickering in gilded lamps;
> Too dim to cross the narrow stream,
> They darken with death's damps.
>
> Home is a haven, the one spot
> Where love and light may reign;
> Where discord may be barred without
> And sweetest peace remain.

Jeremiah.—Pretty sound doctrine, but a little fanciful, I should say. I believe in strict temperance, boys.

Jerusha.—Dear Jeremiah, let us make our home a safer haven.

Jeremiah.—I'm sure I'm willin', if you won't make eternal war against dirt and noise.

Fling.—Mother's going to wage war quietly, that's the idea, and I'll dance on the porch. Hurra! [*Exit Fling.*]

Jerusha.—Leo, son, lie down on the lounge. Jeremiah, dear, take this rocker and the book [*Leo hands it to him*] while I get dinner. [*Exit Jerusha.*]

Jeremiah (*seating himself*).—The millennium is surely come, and home is Heaven.

[CURTAIN FALLS.]

MRS. S. L. OBERHOLTZER.

OUR COUNTRY'S WEALTH.

CHARACTERS.

Six girls. to personify—1, COLUMBIA, dressed as the Goddess of Liberty and seated on a throne; 2, NEW ENGLAND; 3, MIDDLE ATLANTIC STATES; 4, SOUTHERN STATES; 5, STATES OF THE MISSISSIPPI VALLEY; 6, PACIFIC STATES. All dressed in white.

Columbia.—Come hither toward me, my handmaidens, and disclose to my gaze the tribute you have to render unto me, for this year of our Lord, one thousand eight hundred and eighty-five. How sayest thou, New England? What offerings bringest thou? Group of the Middle Atlantic, what good gifts can I claim from you? Dark-eyed, beauteous South, what tribute bearest thou in thy fair palm? Child of energy, Central group, advance and show your contributions. And thou, fair West, daughter of the setting sun, let me behold the glitter of thy annual offering. Each, in turn come hither and reward my tender love for all by duteous display of tribute due. [*With a majestic wave of her hand.*] Advance, New England.

New England (*bearing a piece of granite in her hands, which she places at the feet of Columbia*).—At thy command, O Queen! I draw near. Here is offering rare, digged from the quarries of the "Old Granite State." In massy piles, awaiting thy command, lies the timber, stout and strong, cut from the majestic forests of the North, while from the busy workshops and noisy factories, dotting all the fair land in numbers great, are sent forth a thousand proofs of our toil and enterprise. In thy hands, Oh! gracious sovereign, I lay New England's tribute, with the hope that it meets with thy queenly approval.

Columbia.—Nobly hast thou done, New England! Now let the Middle Atlantic recite her worth and work.

Middle Atlantic (*bringing iron-ore, or bits of coal, in a small, shallow basket*).—Our offering, most gracious Columbia, beloved Queen, we trust is not unworthy of thy acceptance. We have delved into the deep places of the earth, and thence have brought the metal of strength for thy implements of tillage or of warfare, the dusky diamonds whose burning hearts will give thee warmth, and the wonderful oil from its storehouses under the rocks. We bring thee the webs from a thousand looms and the cunning devices from a thousand workshops. We offer thee ships and sailors to transport the work of our hands to the four quarters of the globe and receive thence spices and myrrh and all fair things. O, Queen, canst thou ask more?

Columbia.—Middle Atlantic, right well have you em-

ployed your trust. Accept our queenly commendation **and**
give place to your sister, the South.

*South (presenting a small fruit-basket lined with raw cotton
and filled with oranges).*—Sovereign beloved, the South
salutes thee. In thousands of our cotton fields the bursting pods offer pure white hearts for thy taking. The
juicy canes of lowland acres bring their sweetness for
thy delectation. Rice marshes and orange groves, fruits
and flowers, bring thee greeting. Have I done well, my
liege?

Columbia.—Beloved, I kiss thy hand and murmur
benediction. States of the Centre, where are you?

*Central States (carrying stalks of grain which she presents
to Columbia).*—From prairies wide and river valleys fair
receive the corn and wine which are thy due. Our barns
are bursting with their plenty, our waving plains are evel
murmuring—" Come and take." We also bring to thee
rich stores of metals pure. Copper and lead and iron are
thine, if thou but speak the word. We bring thee cattle
from a thousand hills. Can we do more?

Columbia.—Richly art thou endowed, my daughter, and
bounteously givest thou. Wilt thou now give place to her
who cometh hither from the far Western shore? I would
hear from her.

West (with offering of quartz, or rock to imitate it).—From
world-famed vale of giant trees, from mountain gullies rich
with metals rare, I reach my hands to thee, O, Queen
Columbia. My offering here I bring—silver pale and
yellow gold, and fruits of mammoth growth. The cluster-
ing richness of the vine, we bring thee also. Is not our gift
most fair?

Columbia.—I grant thee grace and approbation real.
Though last, not least art thou. All have done nobly, each

in her place, and here I call you round me. Let me feel
what 'tis to be so well upheld. New England and Middle
at my right, fair South and Central on my left, and thou,
West, my youngest, here at my footstool stand. [*They place
themselves according to Columbia's directions, thus forming a
tableau and singing Columbia, the Gem of the Ocean, audience
joining in the chorus. If preferred, the music may be omitted,
closing simply with the tableau.*

E. CELIA ROOK

THE BEST POLICY.

CHARACTERS.

MR. RATTENBURY, whose bark is worse than his bite.
BOB BOLTER, who only wants to borrow.
JACK JUDSON, a young man of principle.
LITTLE BENNY WARREN, who lost his way.

SCENE.—*A rudely furnished room. Table in centre. Small
stove at right, on which sits a tea-kettle. Rough bed made
of blankets at left. A couple of chairs without backs, on one
of which is tin wash-basin, makes up the rest of the furniture.
Table is set with tin plates and cracked and broken crockery.
Lighted candle in centre. As curtain rises Bob Bolter is
discovered placing a supper on the table from some brown
paper parcels.*

Bob (*cheerily*).—There we are! Some nice cold ham,
some rolls, some mince pie, and [*turning to stove*] if that
fire ever comes up we'll have some coffee. O my, though,
didn't I strike luck to-day? Not any too soon either, for
Jack's without a cent in his pocket and we hadn't a crumb
in the house. Thank Heaven I didn't have to beg! I was

afraid it would come to that—and it would, probably, if I hadn't had the good fortune to get a job shoveling snow off the City Hall sidewalk. It was hard work, to be sure, and cold work, too; but it gave me a dollar and a half which bought me a snow-shovel with which I can earn more to-morrow, and it provided us with a jolly good supper for to-night, too. After all, we're not so bad off! [*Looking about room.*] It's cozy here if it's not luxurious. We're not Vanderbilts nor Jay Goulds and we haven't exactly a palace, but the windows are tight enough to keep the cold out, and so long as we pay our rent— [*Starting suddenly.*] Pay our rent! That's what I never thought of. It's a month overdue now, and unless we raise ten dollars by the time Old Rattlebones comes around again, out we go. Well, my dollar and a half wouldn't have done much in that way, and if he will wait until to-morrow, Jack's wages for the fortnight will be paid to him, and we can pay the rent and have two dollars to spare. It's time Jack was here now. What can be keeping the boy, I wonder? Won't he be jolly glad when he sees the fire and the supper and catches a whiff of that hot coffee! [*Sounds are heard outside.*] Ah! Here he comes now. [*Knock is heard at door, L.*] What does he mean by knocking? Come in!

(*Enter Mr. Rattenbury.*)

Mr. Rattenbury.—Ah! Here you are, are you! Quite warm and snug and comfortable, ain't you?

Bob.—Trying to be, Mr. Rattenbury.

Mr. Rattenbury.—Struck a fortune, I suppose, eh?

Bob.—Not exactly; no, sir.

Mr. Rattenbury.—Well, I'm sorry to hear that.

Bob.—So am I, sir.

Mr. Rattenbury.—I suppose you're glad to see me, and that you have my money waiting for me, eh?

Bob.—Not exactly, Mr. Rattenbury; we haven't the money in hand just now to pay your rent, but if you'll wait—

Mr. Rattenbury (testily).—Wait! Wait! It's always wait. I'm tired of waiting and I won't wait any longer. No sir, not a day longer; not another day, sir. I must have the ten dollars due to-night—this very night—or you'll sleep in a coal-bin or a dry-goods box.

Bob.—To-morrow, Mr. Rattenbury, we'll be able to pay you. My friend Judson will have the money then and you shall have every dollar due you.

Mr. Rattenbury.—Ha! ha! That's an old dodge, Bolter, a very old dodge! We have heard it before, many times before. If you haven't it now, you won't have it then. You can't blind me, young man! Out you go.

Bob.—Can't you take my word, sir?

Mr. Rattenbury.—Pie-crust promises yours are—easily broken, very easily broken. No sir, I can't take any word, money is what I want—money! money! money!

Bob (aside).—What shall I do with Old Rattlebones? I must stave him off for a while, anyhow. [*Aloud.*] Perhaps Judson will bring something home with him when he comes. He will be here soon; will you wait?

Mr. Rattenbury.—No sir, I won't wait; I hate to wait. If I were a joker I'd tell you I'm not a waiter, but I don't feel like joking and so I won't tell you. I'll go away and come back again. I have several other tenants in the neighborhood. I will see them and come back. If the money is not ready then, I shall have to throw this old rubbish of yours into the street and lock your door. Do you understand me?

Bob.—O yes, sir, I understand.

Mr. Rattenbury.—Have the money ready! Have the money ready! [*Exit Mr. Rattenbury, L.*]

Bob (sitting down on chair).—Old Rattlebones seems determined, sure enough. I wonder if he really would throw us out a cold night like this. It strikes me his bark is worse than his bite, and that he's only trying to frighten us. There isn't the least chance in the world of Jack having any money before to-morrow, and there isn't a friend from whom we could borrow a penny, that's a certainty. After all, it looks rather shaky and no mistake. [*Rises, goes to stove, and takes tea-kettle off.*] How's that for a coffee-pot? Not very elegant, but it answers the purpose, and that's all that a silver urn would do. If Jack don't hurry the coffee will be cold, and we won't have time to eat before we're—what is it they call it?—ejected! [*Footsteps heard outside.*] That's Jack, sure enough! Hark! I'm blest if there isn't some one with him, too!

(*Enter Jack, supporting little Ben, L.*)

Jack.—Heigh, ho! What's this? Well, I didn't expect such a cheery reception for my little guest. It's ten hundred times better than I dared to hope.

Bob.—Hello, Jack, old man! Have you brought home company with you? Who is the little shaver?

Jack (leading Little Ben over to stove).—A poor little chap I found asleep and half frozen, in the snow, lying down near the corner of the street. We must get him warmed up, Bob. Thank Heaven! you have a fire. I was not expecting this. You found work, did you?

Bob.—Yes, and not any too soon, either. It wasn't much, to be sure, but it was enough to give us fire and a supper, and small favors must be thankfully received, eh?

Jack (sitting down by stove and rubbing Little Ben's hands).—Do you feel warmer, my little man? [*Little Ben shakes his head affirmatively.*] Is that coffee I smell, Bob?

Bob.—I am happy to say it is.

Jack.—Pour out a cup for the young gentleman, will you?

Bob.—Why, certainly! We haven't any sugar or cream. I hope he will excuse that. [*Pouring out cup of coffee from tea-kettle.*]

Jack.—It will warm him up. [*Gives coffee to Little Ben, who drinks it.*] That's nice and hot, isn't it?

Ben.—Yes, sir. You are very kind to me.

Jack.—Poor little chap, if I hadn't found you, you might have frozen to death.

Bob.—What were you sleeping in the snow for? Don't you know that's a poor sort of a bed?

Ben.—O sir! I was so tired. I had walked so far, and I was so cold, and at last I grew very sleepy. I could not keep my eyes open, and then I don't remember any more until this gentleman 'wakened me.

Jack.—And where did you come from?

Ben.—From grandpa's office, sir.

Bob.—And where were you going?

Ben.—He sent me with twenty dollars to pay a bill, but I lost my way, and I was trying to find it again.

Jack.—And you couldn't, could you?

Ben.—No sir. I asked several people, but I guess they thought I was begging, for they only hurried on and wouldn't stop to listen to me.

Bob.—Are you hungry?

Ben.—Yes sir.

Jack.—Give him something to eat, Bob.

Bob (*getting some bread and ham from table*).—To be sure I will. Here's a sandwich for him. What's his name?

Ben.—Benny Warren, sir.

Jack (*taking sandwich and handing it to him*).—Here, Benny, eat this, and you'll feel better.

Ben (taking sandwich and eating).—Thank you, sir.

Jack.—And when you have had all you want to eat, you shall lie down over there and have a nice nap. And then I will take you home, for I dare say your mamma is very much worried about you now.

Ben (with his mouth full).—Thank you, sir. I should never be able to find my way by myself.

Bob.—Quite a little gentleman, isn't he?

Jack.—That he is. [*Getting up and drawing chair to table.*] I'm rather hungry myself, Bob; suppose we pitch in. There you go, Benny. Trot over there and lie down and rest yourself.

(*Ben lies down on blankets, L., and is soon asleep. Bob and Jack sit at table, Bob left and Jack right. While eating they converse.*)

Bob.—I suppose you brought the rent home with you!

Jack.—The rent? Well, I guess not. There's no drawing money in advance down at our shop. I managed to borrow fifty cents from the foreman with which I meant to buy some supper if you hadn't bought it already, and I considered myself lucky to get that.

Bob.—You see, Old Rattlebones has been here, and he says he won't wait another day for his money.

Jack.—Did you tell him I had work and would pay him as soon as I get my wages?

Bob.—O yes, I told him everything, but he's determined to bounce us.

Jack.—I don't believe he's got the heart.

Bob.—Hasn't he, though? My dear Jack, if we don't raise the money in half an hour, there's no hope for us. We'll either have to throw Old Rattlebones out the window or vamose the ranche, as they say out West.

Jack.—Raise the money? Where on earth are we to raise it?

Bob.—I was just thinking [*pointing significantly to Ben, who lies sleeping*] that we might borrow a ten from his twenty. He'll sleep quiet enough until morning, when you can take him home, explain all about the matter, and pay back the ten when you get your wages to-morrow night. Or his father might give you that as a reward—see?

Jack.—O no, Bob, not that. It would be stealing, my boy. We have no right to touch a penny of the little chap's money. I'll take him home to-night, and maybe they'll give me the reward then.

Bob.—But that will be too late. Old Rattlebones will have been here. [*Steps heard outside.*] Old Rattlebones is here now, and if I'm not mistaken we've either got to mob him or be mobbed.

Jack.—We won't take little Ben's money, that's certain. We must be honest, Bob, under all circumstances.

(*Enter Mr. Rattenbury.*)

Mr. Rattenbury.—So you're in, are you, Judson?

Jack.—You see me, sir.

Mr. Rattenbury.—And you have the money?

Bob.—No sir, we haven't. As I told you, we can't pay you before to-morrow.

Mr. Rattenbury.—Which means next week, next month, next year. Well, you know the consequences. Get out!

Jack.—You're not going to turn us out to-night, Mr. Rattenbury?

Mr. Rattenbury.—Never put off until to-morrow what can be done to-day, that's my motto. Come now, move your furniture. [*Turns to bed. Little Ben is rolled up in covers and cannot be seen.*] Here, I'll carry your bed out for you. [*Stoops down and attempts to drag it out, and in doing so discovers Ben.*] What's this? You've got a boarder, have you? Why don't you get the rent out of him? Is he penniless, too?

Bob.—No sir, he's not penniless. He has twenty dollars in his pocket now, but—

Mr. Rattenbury.—Why don't you borrow it of him?

Jack.—Because, sir, it don't belong to him; he was—

(*Little Ben, who has been awakened by the talking and the pulling at his bed, jumps up and runs to Mr. Rattenbury, who has his back to him.*)

Ben (interrupting).—O grandpa! grandpa! I'm so glad to find you.

Mr. Rattenbury (turning in surprise).—Why Benny, my child, where did you come from? What are you doing here?

Ben.—I lost my way, and this young man took me in and was so kind and good to me.

Jack.—I found him half frozen in the snow, sir.

Mr. Rattenbury.—And did you pay the bill?

Ben.—No sir, I couldn't find the office. I got lost.

Mr. Rattenbury.—And you told these young men all about it and that you were my grandson?

Ben.—O no, sir, I didn't say whose grandson I was. I told them where I lived, and that one [*pointing to Jack*] was going to take me home this evening.

Mr. Rattenbury.—Well, it's fortunate they found you. Poor child, I ought to have known better than to send you on an errand this cold weather, but I hadn't an idea but that you could find the place.

Bob.—And he's your grandson, is he, sir?

Mr. Rattenbury.—He is, yes. I must thank you for being so good to him.

Jack.—O don't mention it, sir.

Mr. Rattenbury.—And you wouldn't borrow ten dollars of the money you knew he had, even to save yourselves from being thrown out into the street?

Bob.—I wanted to borrow it, but Jack persuaded me it wouldn't be honest.

Mr. Rattenbury.—And Jack was right. He deserves credit; you both deserve credit. And I mean to give it to you in more senses than one. Never mind about the rent now. Pay me when you get it. I know I can trust you. I ask your pardon for mistrusting you before. Come to my office in the morning, both of you. I think I can put you in a way to earn a good living where your honesty will be appreciated.

Jack. }
Bob. } —Thank you, sir.

Mr. Rattenbury.—And now, Benny boy, come along home with grandpa; your friends shall be rewarded.

Ben.—Good-bye!

Jack. }
Bob. } —Good-bye, Benny.

Mr. Rattenbury (stopping on threshold).—Young men, you are on the right track. While you are honest, you are sure to succeed.

(*Exit Mr. Rattenbury, L., leading Ben.*)

Bob.—He's not such a bad sort, is he?

Jack.—No, he's not! Old Rattlebones is a brick.

Bob.—And honesty is—

Jack.—The best policy.

[CURTAIN.]

CHARLES STOKES WAYNE.

UNCLE MORTON'S GIFT.

CHARACTERS.

ARTHUR JACKSON, a boy of twelve.
JIMMIE WHITE, a poor boy.
ALICE JACKSON, a young lady.
LUCIE JACKSON, a girl of fourteen.
SILVIE MEREDITH, a friend of Alice's.
ANNIE CARTER, a sewing girl.
SUSIE CARTER, a little invalid girl.
BRIDGET DOLIN, an Irish fruit seller.

COSTUMES.

ALICE, SILVIE, LUCIE, and ARTHUR well and tastefully dressed in the fashion of the day. ANNIE CARTER and SUSIE in faded calico dresses and much-worn shoes. MRS. DOLIN, short calico dress, green gingham apron, large, rough shoes, and a very small plaid shawl pinned over her head.

SCENE I.

Nicely furnished sitting-room. Alice sitting at R. reading. Lucie and Arthur at a table near C., playing checkers.

Arthur.—There's one thing I can't understand.

Alice.—Only one, I suppose?

Arthur.—Of course! And that is—

Lucie (slyly).—How the molasses candy disappeared from the shelf in the closet so mysteriously?

Arthur.—Maybe I know more about that than you think, Miss Lucie. But you're wrong. Guess again.

Lucie.—Is it why Uncle Morton doesn't send us our New Year's money?

Arthur.—I declare, Lu., you've hit it! Say now, Alice, don't you think it's a little queer? Here it is the fifth, and he has always sent it in time for New Year's Day before, you know.

Lucie.—Perhaps he is sick.

Alice.—A hundred things might happen to delay the

mail between here and San Francisco. [*A loud ring is heard.*]

Arthur.—There's the postman now. I'll go and see if he has our letters. [*Goes out, returning in a moment with letters in his hand.*] Hurrah! here they are at last. [*Reads*] Miss Alice Jackson, Miss Lucie Jackson, Master Arthur Morton Jackson. What'll you give for them, girls?

Alice (holding out her hand).—Now don't tease, Arthur. Give me mine, please.

Arthur (handing one to Alice and another to Lucie).—There, calm yourselves, ladies. You know exactly what's in them. How unfortunate it is to be the youngest of the family. [*Opening his letter and unfolding a check.*] Here I have only twelve dollars, while Alice has—let me see [*peeps over her shoulder*]—twenty! My gracious, Alice, but you're getting old.

Lucie.—I just wish I was twenty instead of fourteen! Fourteen dollars will buy lots of things that I want, but twenty—only think of having twenty dollars all at once!

(*Enter Silvie Meredith.*)

Silvie.—Ann told me you were all up here, so I took the liberty of coming right up.

Alice (rising and kissing her).—I am so glad to see you, Silvie. It is such a long time since you were here last.

Silvie.—I have been away three weeks.

Arthur and Lucie.—I didn't see you at first. How do you do?

Lucie.—I'm well, thank you.

Arthur.—So am I, considering the circumstances.

Silvie.—What circumstances?

Arthur.—Why, Christmas and New Year's, you know, and having two young ladies ordering me about from morn-

ing till night. It's "Arthur, won't you please do this?"
"Arthur, do stop that!" "Arthur dear, won't you please
run down town for me?"

Alice (laughing).—Oh, yes, you are dreadfully abused.

Lucie.—What an absurd boy you are! It isn't half so
bad as he makes it out, Miss Silvie.

Alice.—Come over here and sit down, Silvie. I want to
ask you something. You can go on with your game, children. [*Alice and Silvie sit down.*]

Lucie (sarcastically).—Children!

(*Lucie and Arthur resume their seats at the table, but listen
to what Silvie and Alice are saying.*)

Alice (to Silvie).—You know our Uncle Morton always
sends us each a present of money at New Year's to corres-
pond with our ages.

Silvie.—That is very kind and generous of him, I think.

Arthur.—Oh, he don't hurt himself. He's as rich as
Croesus.

Alice.—Mine is twenty dollars this year, and I'm won-
dering just what I had better do with it. Of course, I
want to get the greatest amount of satisfaction out of it
that I can. There's a lovely engraving of Guido's
"Mater Dolorosa" at Norman's. I can't decide whether
to get that or an elegantly bound edition of Shakespeare
I saw at Randall's.

Lucie.—Well, I know what I want without any trouble.
I have set my heart on a monkey-skin collar and muff.
They have been reduced since the holidays, and I can get
a lovely set at Arnold's for fifteen dollars.

Arthur.—Oh, what queer things you girls are! I'm the
only one who has a sensible plan. I'm going to buy a
printing press. Will you give me an order for some cards,
Miss Silvie?

Silvie.—Perhaps so.

Alice.—Now, which would you rather have if you were I, Silvie?—Shakespeare, or the " Mater Dolorosa "?

Silvie.—I fear I should find it hard to decide between the two, they are both so tempting. But, as there is no pressing need of your deciding at once, I wish you would come and take a walk with me. There's a picture I want you to see that you may possibly feel more like spending your money for than the " Mater Dolorosa " even.

Alice.—What can it be? I am very anxious to see it. Shall we go now?

Silvie.—Yes, if you please. The afternoons are so short, you know. [*Turns to Lucie.*] Lucie, may I go with you to-morrow morning to look at the furs you are going to buy?

Lucie.—Yes, indeed, I should be ever so glad to have you.

Arthur.—Look here, this isn't fair. Don't you want me to escort you somewhere?

Silvie.—I certainly do, Arthur. If you will come round to my house at three o'clock to-morrow I will very gladly avail myself of your kind offer.

Arthur.—All right, I'll be there.

SCENE II.

A plainly furnished room. Annie sitting at R. sewing. Susie lying on lounge, L. Silvie and Alice in out-door wraps sitting near C.

Silvie.—Are you working as hard as usual, Annie?

Annie.—Yes, miss. I get up at six in the morning and I'm seldom in bed again before midnight.

Alice.—But you don't sew steadily all that time, surely?

Annie.—Yes, I do, miss. It's the only way I can make

anything, and even then I only make enough to keep us barely comfortable. Susie is so delicate and her appetite is so poor that I have to buy some nice little things to tempt her to eat at all sometimes. If she were strong and well like other children it would be different. I have to be so careful of her. If I should lose her I shouldn't want to live any longer.

Silvie.—But if you work in this way you will certainly kill yourself, and then what would become of little Susie? Can't you get anything to do but those coarse shirts?

Annie.—I have tried, but so far I have failed. I don't like to take time to go and look for work, for every hour means a few cents at least, and I'm sure of getting my pay for these, if it is small. If I could only lay by a little, I should have some hope, but it is so discouraging to spend every cent as fast as you get it. I don't mean to complain, but when I think how it used to be when mother and father were alive I can scarcely bear it. We had such a comfortable, pleasant little home, and I knew almost nothing of what care was. But now—[*weeps.*]

Silvie (*rising and laying her hand on Annie's shoulder*).— Oh, don't cry, Annie. There are brighter days in store for you, I am sure. Indeed, I can assure you there is a rift in the clouds already. I will give you some sewing to do for me, and I am sure I can interest others for you.

Alice.—I have some work at home that I have been putting off for want of leisure. I shall be only too glad to have you do it for me if you will.

Annie.—Indeed I will, and thank you very, very much.

Alice (*to Susie*).—What do you do to amuse yourself all day long?

Susie (*shyly*).—I sit at the window and look out sometimes. Sometimes I play with my doll. [*Shows a stick with an apron tied around it.*] Sometimes sister and I tell each other stories, but most times I make pictures.

Alice.—Make pictures? How?

Susie.—Sister bought me a pencil and some nice, smooth brown paper, and I make trees and houses and little girls and boys and dogs and cats and horses and everything I can think of.

Alice.—Suppose you could have just whatever you wanted, what would you like?

Susie (to Annie).—Shall I tell her, sister?

Annie.—Of course, dear, since the lady is so kind as to ask you.

Susie.—If I could have a box of paints, so I could paint my pictures, I should be just as happy as I could be.

Alice.—Then you may begin to be happy now, for you shall have them. And suppose you could have a doll with red cheeks and blue eyes and real yellow curls, how would you like that?

Susie.—Oh, dear me. I'm afraid I'd cry, I'd be so happy.

Alice.—Well, you may look for one before night. And now, Silvie, don't you think we are making our call very long?

Silvie.—Yes, we must go. Now, Annie, after you have finished that set of shirts, don't get any more. You shall have better work and better pay than you have had. Good-bye.

Annie.—Good-bye, Miss Meredith. I don't know how to thank you for all your kindness to Susie and me.

SCENE III.

The street. A corner fruit-stand, with oranges, apples, figs, and nuts arranged upon it. Bridget Dolin sitting beside it.
(Enter Silvie and Lucie.)

Silvie.—Will you object to stopping a moment, Lucie? I want to speak to this woman.

Lucie.—Do you know her, Miss Silvie?

Silvie.—I buy fruit of her quite often. You will find her very interesting, I think. Good-morning, Mrs. Dolin.

Mrs. D.—Sure, an' is it yerself, miss? The top of the mornin' till yez!

Silvie.—Thank you. Please give me a dozen oranges.

Mrs. D.—Wid all me heart, miss, an' blessin's on ye for the shwate young leddy that ye are! It's the first sale I've had the morn, an' I was just gettin' a bit down-hearted like.

Silvie.—I thought you didn't get down-hearted, Mrs. Dolin?

Mrs. D.—No more I don't, miss, unless I jist can't help it. [*Wipes her eyes on her apron.*]

Silvie.—Has anything gone wrong at home?

Mrs. D.—Wrong, is it? Sure, an' it seems as if everything in the wurruld war turruned upside down wid me! Arrah, but it's an angel ye are, jist to be inquirin' into the throubles o' the likes o' me! But since ye're axin, I'll tel! yez the thruth. There isn't a livin' man as could be betther nor me own Pathrick whin the dhrink isn't intil him. It's yerself knows I've said that same thing to yea many's the time. But onct he gets a dhrop o' the craythur, he's jist wild like. It's mesilf belaves he don't know what he's about at all, at all. He got home afore me lasht night, an' he bated little Tim so that the poor child's flat on his back the day wid every bone in him achin'. An Maggie, she's in bed wid a fayver like, though the docthor says there's no inflection about it. An' Molly fell agin the shtove yestherday an' burruned her poor airm to a blisher. So ye see, miss, we're in a peck o' throuble intirely.

Silvie.—Indeed, I should think so. I am very sorry. May I go to your house this afternoon and see if I can do anything for the children, Mrs. Dolin?

Mrs. D.—May yez, is it? Jist listen till her, now! Dade, miss, they couldn't be more pleased to see your shwate face if ye was a blissed angel from heaven! It's meself wad like to be there this minute, lookin' afther the poor things; but if I was to shtay wid thim, where wad I be afther gettin' the money to kape a dacint roof over their heads, not to mintion the bit dhresses an' jackets an' sich like, an' the bread an' praties they has to ate.

Lucie.—You may give me a dozen oranges and a pound of figs, Mrs. Dolin.

Mrs. D. (beginning to do them up).—Faith, it's a fine young leddy ye are, miss! I hope ye'll find thim as shwate as honey.

Lucie.—Don't you find it very cold sitting here with nothing but that little shawl over your head? I should think you would freeze.

Mrs. D.—Dade, miss, I think I shall some o' these days Sure I couldn't shtand it at all, at all, if I didn't jist kape thinkin' o' the childher.

Silvie.—I think we will go, now, Lucie. Good-morning Mrs. Dolin.

Lucie.—Good-morning.

Mrs. D.—The same to ye both, an' may every mornin' be betther and betther as long as ye live !

Scene IV.

A very bare room. Pine table, a wooden chair, a three-legged stool, a small, rusty stove with no fire in it. An old bedstead or settee in one corner covered with faded patch-work quilt. Jimmie White lying thereon with an old picturebook and some pieces of broken toys beside him. A knock is heard.

Jimmie.—Come in.

(*Enter Silvie and Arthur.*)

Silvie (going to bedside).—Well, Jimmie, how are you to-day? Is the pain in your back very bad?

Jimmie.—Yes'm, pretty bad, but not so bad as it is sometimes.

Silvie.—I have brought a friend of mine to see you. His name is Arthur Jackson. Arthur, this is Jimmie White.

Arthur (shaking hands with Jimmie).—I say, old chap, do you have to lie here all the time?

Jimmie.—Oh, yes.

Arthur.—Well, now, I call that tough. Who looks after you?

Jimmie.—My mother does. But she goes out to work for folks when she can get anything to do, and then I have to stay here alone.

Arthur.—Don't you get lonesome?

Jimmie.—Awful lonesome.

Arthur.—I see you've got a book there. Do you like to read?

Jimmie.—I'd read all the time if I could get anything to read. My mother finds an old newspaper sometimes, and once the folks where she was workin' gave her this old picturebook.

Arthur.—What do you have to eat?

Jimmie.—Potatoes and bread and once in a while some soup. Christmas Day we had some meat, but I couldn't eat it.

Arthur.—Don't you ever have rice or farina or oranges or grapes or figs or jelly or cocoa or anything nice?

Jimmie.—My! I guess not! We're too poor to buy such things.

Arthur.—Gracious! If I can't have everything of that kind when I'm sick, I think it's pretty hard times. But look here, Jimmie, your fire's all gone out! Don't you want me to make one for you? I should think you'd freeze to death. This room is as cold as a barn. Where is your coal and kindling-wood and shavings?

Jimmie.—There ain't any.

Arthur.—My stars and garters! If that don't beat me. Look here, young fellow. You wouldn'ts'pose I could carry coal and wood and blankets and books and good things to eat in my pocket, would you? But I can, though. Miss Silvie, shall I escort you to one of the stores around the corner, or will you wait here till I come for you?

Silvie.—I think I'll go now. Good-bye, Jimmie.

Jimmie.—Good-bye.

SCENE V.

The Jacksons' sitting-room. Enter Silvie, Alice, Lucie, Arthur.

Alice.—Oh, Silvie! I'm afraid you are very artful. What a cunning plot you laid for us all.

Silvie (laughing).—You needn't have fallen into it so easily as you did. I didn't ask you to buy dresses and shoes and cloaks and color-boxes for Annie Carter and her sister. Lucie had Mrs. Dolin bundled up in a warm

hood and shawl, and every one of the little Dolins provided with woolen stockings and a pair of shoes almost
before I knew what she was about. And the way Arthur
whisked me in and out of one store after another to get
the things for Jimmie White! You would have thought
he had a hundred dollars at his command instead of
twelve.

Arthur.—Wasn't it fun, though, Miss Silvie?

Silvie.—Yes, indeed it was. You see, Alice, I have become interested in these poor people. But, you know, I
haven't much money of my own, so I thought I could at
least give you the chance of doing what I would do myself
if I could.

Alice.—To be serious, Silvie, I am heartily glad that
you did give us such a chance. I was never so thoroughly
satisfied as I am now with the way I used Uncle Morton's
gift.

Lucie.—Nor I.

Arthur.—Nor I. It was regularly jolly. And now,
girls, I move we give Miss Silvie a vote of thanks, and
that we all enjoy ourselves in the same way next year.
All in favor say aye.

Alice and Lucie.—Aye!

Arthur.—The ayes have it.

[CURTAIN FALLS.]

LILIAN F. WELLS.

THE OPENING ADDRESS.

CHARACTERS.

JACK, TOM, and DAN.

SCENE I.

The speech in preparation.

Jack (*soliloquizing*).—Well, I am in a fix—a decided fix. Here's Exhibition Day close at hand, and I am expected to deliver the "Opening Address," and I have no more idea what to say than "the man in the moon." Let me see! I must try to make up something for the occasion. [*Looking around.*] There doesn't seem to be any one around, so I think I'll have a little private rehearsal in the solitude of these grand old woods. I believe it is customary in these opening addresses first to make a profound bow [*bows*], and then to commence something like this: Ladies and gentlemen, we are glad to welcome you here to this, our annual entertainment, and we hope—we hope—and we hope— [*Commences again in a louder tone.*] Ladies and gentlemen, we are glad to welcome you here to this our annual entertainment, and we hope—we hope—

Dan (*who has entered with Tom, unperceived*).—And we hope that you are not taking leave of your senses, Jack.

Tom.—Nor contemplating going on the stage—

Dan.—Nor suffering from an attack of brain fever. But really, Jack, I am afraid we startled you. You look frightened and a little sheepish, too. Do tell us what you were doing, that's a good fellow.

Tom.—Yes, where are all those ladies and gentlemen whom you were addressing? And what is it you hope to do? There's some joke ahead, I know, and you may as well own up.

Jack.—Well, I will; and although it may seem a joke to you, I assure you it's anything but a joke to me. I never felt more serious in my life than I do this minute.

Tom.—If that's the case, maybe we can do something for you.

Dan.—Yes, give us the chance to be the "friends in need," won't you, Jack?

Jack (brightening).—That's so! I believe you are the very fellows to help me out of this fix. I wonder that I did not think of it before. But "three heads are better than one," you know. Well, then, to tell the truth, boys, I was trying to compose a little opening speech for our school entertainment to-morrow afternoon, and after the first stereotyped sentence, I got hopelessly lost; but here you are to help me out of the maze, and set me on my feet again.

Dan.—Is that all your trouble? Then cease to groan, for Tom and I will set you right in a few minutes. We know all about it, for we've been through the mill, haven't we, Tom?

Tom.—That we have! and if you will take our advice, Jack, and act upon some hints that we will give you, I will venture to assert that you will get through with your speech famously, and will sit down amid such deafening applause that you will begin to feel as though you were a born Demosthenes with a great and glorious future before you.

Dan.—Yes, and you will wonder how it was that you or your friends had not discovered these signs of genius before.

Jack.—Oh, I'm not quite so conceited as all that, boys, but I am really anxious to hear your suggestions, as I have not yet one good idea.

Tom.—Well, then, we will proceed at once to business

When you get up to make your speech, Jack, you must look neither to the right nor the left, but gaze blankly ahead at nothing; and when you feel your heart rising up in your throat, and a mist coming over your eyes and a weakness into your knees, make a tremendous effort to appear perfectly at ease, and your audience will never suspect that you are standing upon "pins and needles," wishing that something would happen to hide you from their gaze.

Dan.—And then, when you feel the " silence of death " around you, commence with your " Ladies and gentlemen, we are glad to welcome you here to this our school anniversary, and we hope that our exercises at this time will meet with your approbation and will prove to you that we are making earnest efforts to improve our time and opportunities. And although we do not expect to become Platos or Ciceros, yet we do hope to grow into wise and useful men, exerting an influence for the good of mankind in whatsoever station of life we may be placed."

Tom.—Then bring in the plea about your extreme youth, you know, something like this: " Many of us are very young, and therefore we ask you not to criticise too harshly any mistakes or imperfections that you may notice at this time. We hope that as we grow older our wisdom will increase with our years, and that the knowledge we are daily gaining in the school-room will better prepare us to meet the stern realities of life when they are presented to us."

Dan.—And then, when you have quoted the favorite expression that has been put into the mouths of all the sage little orators in our big country, namely—" Where should we look for our future statesmen and Presidents but to the public schools of our own beloved America ?"—then, I say, when you have have said this in a solemn and impressive manner, you can proceed to wind up your address with thanks to the audience for their attendance.

Jack.—And with some remarks about the exercises that are to follow. Yes, I think I can do that part all right. And now I'll go and think over the speech and fix it just as I mean to say it on the stage to-morrow afternoon.

Tom.—And we'll be on hand, Jack, to help you bear your honors.

Jack.—All right. I'm off now to prepare my speech.

[CURTAIN.]

SCENE II.

The speech.

Jack.—Ladies and gentlemen, we are glad to welcome you here to this our school anniversary, and we hope that our exercise—our sexercise [*he begins to get excited—wipes his face and runs his hands through his hair*]—our serexcises at this time will meet with your approbation and will prove—will prove that you are making—that is, that you are trying to make—or, rather, to improve—your time and opportunities. And although we do not expect—do not expect—er—we do not expect—er-ate to become Catos and Pliceros, yet we hope to grow—to grow—up—[*in a desperate tone, and mopping his face violently*] to grow till we are grown up—thereby exhorting in affluence for the good of men-kind, in whatever life in the station-house we may be p'liced. Many of us are very young—many of us are very young and some of us are very young—yes, many of you are mere babes—and therefore we ask you not to criticise too harshly any mismakes that you may take at this or any other time. Therefore—we hope as you grow—bigger—our age will increase with our years, and that the

marbles we are daily gaining in the school-yard will prepare us the better for the real sternalities of life when
they—when they [*gesturing wildly*]—when they—therefore—where should we look for our future fratesmen and
stesidents but to the scublic pools of our be-lown loved
America? We thank you for your attendance here and we
hope—we do hope—that you will enjoy the fleeches that
are to spollow—which are worse if not better than the one
you have just heard—I mean—that is—which are better if
not worse than the one I have just heard. [*Retires in con-
fusion.*]

L. J. AND E. C. ROOK.

HAVE A SHINE, SAH?

CHARACTERS.

BOOTBLACK.   COUNTRYMAN.
NEWSBOY.   DUDE.
                    POLICEMAN.

SCENE, ON THE STREET.—*Bootblack and Newsboy standing
on the street. Bootblack with his kit and brush ready for
action. Newsboy well supplied with papers. Enter Countryman in very old-fashioned clothing and coarse boots.*

Newsboy (addressing Countryman).—Papers, boss? Times,
Press, Herald, Record. All the latest news. Bank robbery in New York. Jolly elopement. Pictures of the
man to be hung to-morrow in six positions; best that can
be got! [*Displaying a pictured paper.*] Only two cents,
sir. Have a copy?

Bootblack.—Shine, sah? Hab yer boots shined?

Countryman (spurning the offered papers).—Clear the
track wi' yer papers! I've got an almanac, I reckon.

Newsboy (*taking a step backward*).—Better have a paper, boss! All the latest news.

Bootblack.—Hab a shine, sah? [*Flourishing his brush.*] Gib yer boots a lubly shine, massa.

Countryman.—Don't kere if I do, seein' ye're so willin.' It'll tickle Martha. She says boots oughter be black. I mos'ly use lard-ile, that's best. But len' me yer brush, youngster.

Bootblack (*placing his kit in position to receive the heavy boot*).—Sot yer foot up yer, sah.

Countryman (*using the kit as a boot-jack*).—I swan, this thing ain't half so good as the stair door to pull off a feller's boot! 'Taint got no hold, no how! [*Kicking it over.*]

Bootblack.—Whoa, sah? yer spillen ob de blacknen an opsottin' ob de kit. Dar, massa, sot up yer hansum boot, somewise so. [*Lifting the booted foot to position on the kit.*]

Countryman.—What comes next? [*Shaking his foot restlessly.*]

Bootblack.—I shines him up lubly, sah. You does de holden still. [*Applies the brush.*]

Countryman.—Great stars! you shine 'em an' don't pull 'em off! When I grease 'em, I allers puts 'em on me hand and roasts it in.

(*Enter Dude, dressed in the most approved dudish style.*)

Bootblack (*looking up from his polishing and doffing his worn hat to the Dude*).—Hab a shine, sah? Jus' a moment ob delay. [*Rubbing rapidly at the Countryman's boot.*]

(*Dude swings his cane and walks loftily.*)

Newsboy.—Papers, mister? Herald, Times, Press, World, Ledger, Record. All the latest sensations!

Dude (*pausing and raising his eye-glasses, with a drawl*). —Ah leave ah World ah and ah Press at ah numba fourteen.

Newsboy.—Yes, sir. Five cents, mister!

Dude.—Ah, ah! [*With some difficulty finding his pocket and the change.*] The ahnoyance and insignifahcance of change!

Bootblack (*to Countryman, as he gives his boot a finishing polish*).—Dat hab a lubly shine now, massa. You 'spect him jus' a moment till I sees dis gen'lman.

(*Countryman takes his foot down awkardly and continues to gaze with amazement at the Dude, twisting his neck to see the wonder in different positions.*)

(*Bootblack, with a quick movement, sets his kit beside the Dude.*)

Dude (*to Newsboy, as he gives him the pennies for papers*).—Deliver the papers ahmediately, boy.

Newsboy.—Yes, sir.

(*Newsboy moves to the side of the stage and employs himself arranging his stock of papers, counting his change, and examining the contents of his pockets.*)

Bootblack (*looking up and down the street, to Dude*).—Dar amn't a gall in sight, massa. I-I be lookin' sharp. Hab a small shine? [*Flourishing his brush.*]

Dude (*raising his glasses and looking up and down the street*).—Ah! yes. [*Putting his small and finely polished boot on the kit.*] Whisk ah the dust with ah delicate brush.

(*Bootblack jerks a fine, light brush from his pocket, with which he rapidly dusts the boot a moment, Dude meanwhile holding his eye-glasses and peering up and down the street.*)

Bootblack.—Dar, dat's lublier dan a mirror. Now, gib me de uder, massa!

Dude.—Ah! [*Exchanging the position of the feet.*]

Bootblack (*rubbing a moment*).—Now dat am handsomer dan nothen.

(*Dude removes his foot, strokes down his tights, and assumes an erect, superb attitude.*)

(*Bootblack doffs his cap and quickly sets his kit beside the
awestruck Countryman.*)

Newsboy (*moving a step or two forward, to Dude*).—
Yer pardon, mister! Any special orders fur to-morrer!
Great news of the execution an other embezzlein to be in
World, Press, Herald, Record, Times, Tribune. Great run
on these papers.

Dude.—Ah! [*Readjusting his glasses and toying with
his watch chain.*] I thought you had ah gone. You may
leave me ah Press and ah Times ahmedially to-morrow.
[*With increased drawl.*] Ahmedially, remember.

Newsboy.—I deliver quicker 'an wink, mister. [*Walks
rapidly off the stage.*]

Bootblack (*who had been waiting a moment or two with his
kit beside the Countryman, who appeared too fully overawed
by the Dude to notice his presence*).—Massa, pleas' sot up
dat uder boot till I shine um.

(*Exit Dude, with a leisurely gait, swinging his cane.*)

Countryman (*in a rather hushed tone*).—What kind o'
critter was that, Darkie? [*Lifting his unpolished boot
slightly.*]

Bootblack.—Sot um boot, so! [*Assisting it to position on
the kit.*] Which, massa? [*Rubbing the boot vigorously.*]

Countryman.—Why, that there crane or whatever ye
call sich animals; that 'mazin' curious thing with spindle
shanks and cocked up head what ye jus' shined. Do they
often come inter town?

Bootblack (*grinning as he rubs*).—Oh, dat were a man,
sah. Dudes da call um. Regular cus'mers when dar no
galls out. I sees lots o' um.

Countryman.—You don't stuff me with no sich yarn!

They're scarce as pizin', I'll vow. Barnum's been burned out agin, sure as ye live, an' this thing's got loose. The queerest critter I ever sot eyes on! Them boots is getten to shine like Sambo.

Bootblack (*applying the brush more rapidly*).—Hab to charge yer double price, sah. Day's mighty hard tu shine.

Countryman (*surprised*).—What's that grumblin' 'bout charge?

Bootblack.—Ten cents, massa, when I'se done. Day's 'mazin' hard to shine.

Countryman (*jerking down his foot*).—Git out! Nobody hired you fur this job. I'd enough sooner hav a layer uf decent grease on me boots. Make a fellow stick here half an hour on one leg an' rub a clean dollar's worth of leather off his boots, then tax im ten cents fur it. No you don't! [*Kicking the kit over.*] Git out! [*Kicking toward the Bootblack.*]

[*Enter Policeman quietly.*]

Bootblack (*affrighted, backing off*).—Please, sah, don't trable on me brushes and smash um box.

Countryman (*to Bootblack*).—I'll shine ye! rubbin' all the grease and leather off a man's boot an' clamin' pay fur the distruction of it. I'll knock yer box inter kindlen wood. [*Giving the kit a pound with the heel of his boot.*]

Policeman (*taking the Countryman's arm*).—Better come along with me, friend, and leave the boy to his trade.

Countryman (*resisting*).—Not much! You cum with me, if there's any cumin' done. [*Policeman and Countryman scuffle quickly off the stage.*]

Bootblack (*grins at their exit, sighs while gathering up his scattered possessions, puts his brush and blacking in the kit*).— Dar am many hard ways ob gettin' an' not gettin' a liben.

[Curtain falls.]

Mrs. S. L. Oberholtzer.

BOLD FOR THE RIGHT.

CHARACTERS.

HARRY STEVENS.　　　EDDIE TAYLOR.　　　JACK WILSON.

Enter Harry from one side of platform and Eddie from the other, meeting in the middle. Harry carries school books in a strap. Eddie has book pushed up under his jacket, which is buttoned over it.

Harry.—Hello, Eddie! Where are you going?

Eddie (in mysterious manner).—Don't say anything, Harry, but the fact is I'm not going to school to-day. I'm going to play hooky!

Harry.—I'm sorry to hear it, Eddie. It's not altogether right, you know. What did you do with your books?

Eddie.—Here they are. [*Showing them under jacket.*] I'm going down to the creek to see Jack Wilson, and then I'm going in swimming. No school for me, a nice day like this.

Harry.—See Jack Wilson, did you say? Where are you going to find him? Has he come home?

Eddie.—Didn't you know? He came back to town last night. There's a crowd of us fellows going down to meet him this morning. He's sure to be down by old Peter's boat-house, and we're going to get him to tell us all about his voyage. Won't you come along, Harry?

Harry.—I'm afraid I can't, Eddie. You see—

Eddie.—O you're afraid of a whipping, are you? Well, then, you'd better not come. Jack don't like cowards.

Harry.—No, I'm not afraid of a whipping at all, but I wouldn't like to deceive mother. She always says she can trust me, and I always want her to say that. I'd like first rate to see Jack, but I won't play truant to see him or any-body else.

Eddie.—What a good boy you are! It's not the first time I've hooked it, and it won't be the last, either. I don't like being cooked in a school-room these warm days. It's much better fun to swim down there below the boat-house. The water's just as clear as crystal, and you don't know how cool and pleasant it makes you feel for the rest of the day. Better come, Harry. You can hide your books under the hedge over there and get them as you go back.

Harry.—But then I shall miss to-day's lessons, and that will throw me back, and you know I want to be number one next month.

Eddie.—Well, if you'd rather be number one than enjoy a swim, you'd better go to school. I'm not ambitious that way. The last bench is just as comfortable as the first one, I think.

Harry.—I wonder if one day would make much differ-ence?

Eddie.—No, of course it wouldn't. You could easily catch up. Besides, that other little fellow is sure to make half a dozen bad misses before the month's out, and you can walk ahead of him. Tell your mother you didn't feel well and thought some fresh air would do you good.

Harry.—But I do feel well.

Eddie.—O you're too particular altogether. However, if you're not coming I must go, because if I don't hurry I may miss Jack, and I want to hear the story he has to tell about meeting the " Flying Dutchman," the phantom ship, you know.

Harry.—Is he going to tell about that?

Eddie.—O yes, and the boys say he can spin sailors' yarns like an old salt. You'd better come !

Harry.—Shall I? No! It's a big temptation, but I won't yield to it, Eddie. School is the place for me.

Eddie.—All right, then. I'll tell Jack how much you think of him. O my, won't he laugh when I tell him that Harry Stevens was afraid to play truant, because he thought his mother might find it out and whip him for it? Jack will enjoy that!

(*Enter Jack quietly. He overhears last remark.*)

Jack.—Laugh, will he, Eddie? Enjoy it, will he? Well, maybe the Jack who ran away might; but the Jack who returned won't. His year's voyage has taught him what a foolish, silly, wicked boy he was to play truant, neglect his studies, and disobey his poor old mother, who died while he was away.

Eddie.—O never mind preaching, Jack, come down—

Jack.—Not yet, Eddie. I don't wonder you are ashamed of yourself and want to get away. Don't you know it was very wrong of you to think of stopping away from school yourself? I hope you're sorry for it. And don't you know it was still more wrong to try to persuade Harry to do so, and then to ridicule him because he had the courage to say " No "?

Eddie.—O, I don't care.

Jack.—But you ought to care, and you will care some day—just as I do now.

Harry.—I think he cares, Jack; but he don't like to own it. He will come and go to school with me after all, I think.

Eddie.—Well, if Jack won't spin any yarns, I suppose I might as well.

Jack.—Jack's yarns shall be spun after school hours to those who answered the roll call and to no others. There now, run away, both of you, and remember always that there is nothing brave or manly or smart in outwitting father, mother, or teacher. The truant seldom comes to any good, and the idle scholar regrets his idleness during all the days of his life. Take Harry as your model, Eddie, and when bad boys ask you to do what you know to be wrong, then be truly brave and manly and bold for the right, and say "No," and stick to it. Will you try?

Eddie.—Yes, I'll try!

Harry.—And now hurry, or we shall both be late. [*Exit Harry and Eddie one way and Jack the other.*]

CHARLES STOKES WAYNE.

THE ART CRITIC.

CHARACTERS.

AUNT NANCY, a quaint old lady in quaint costume.
ISABEL, her niece, a girl of twelve or fourteen years in modern attire.

SCENE.—*An ordinary sitting-room. Aunt Nancy, seated, knitting a stocking. Enter Isabel with portfolio of engravings.*

Isabel.—Auntie, I think you must be tired of that everlasting knit, knit, knit, so come, put your stocking away and look at these pictures I have brought down to show you.

Aunt Nancy.—Yes, child, jest wait till I get my glasses on, and I'll look at your picters as long as you want me to. [*Puts on her spectacles.*]

Isabel.—What do you think of this? It is an engraving from a painting by one of the great masters—I cannot recall his name just now—and I think it very fine.

Aunt N.—Yes, that is fine, and I shouldn't wonder a bit if old Solomon Doolittle drawed that. He was the greatest master I ever knowed, and I tell you, the boys and gals that went to his skule was 'most afeared to wink their eyes when he was around. And he was a powerful hand with the pen and pencil; yes, I wouldn't be afeared to bet my last dollar that this picter is his work.

Isabel.—No, Auntie, that cannot be! But here's something you will appreciate, I'm sure—the Madonna, after Raphael.

Aunt N.—Madonner! It seems to me I've heerd that name afore. Any relation of yourn, Isabel?

Isabel.—Hardly, Aunt Nancy.

Aunt N.—She's a purty creetur. Turns her eyes up a leetle too much, but she's kind o' peaceful lookin'. I like her picter real fust-rate.

Isabel.—I thought you would. Do you like animals?

Aunt N.—Yes, well enough in their places. My! that looks jest like some of Deacon Sly's pesky critters. Shouldn't wonder if they was his.

Isabel.—That is one of Bonheur's animals.

Aunt N.—Bonyur? I don't know him, never saw his animals, neither, but if that's a photograph of 'em, I wouldn't be afeared to set Deacon Sly's agin 'em any day [*Picks up another.*] What's this?

Isabel.—That's a rural scene. You'll like that, I know.

Aunt N.—Do tell! Jest look at that pig-pen, it's as nateral as life, and there's the pig, too. It reminds me of your Uncle Josh, he was so fond of pork.

Isabel.—Do you see the mountains in the distance, Auntie, and the soft, beautiful clouds above them?

Aunt N.—Yes, I see 'em, but they're not as purty to my eyes as the pigs and the chickens and the turkeys. Take it away, it makes me feel kind o' homesick.

Isabel.—Here's an ocean view. I think this is exquisite.

Just look at the waste of waters, and only this strip of beach as a foreground.

Aunt N.—Well, of all things—where's the picter? That's about as near nothin' as the leetle end of a pinted stick. Why, there's nothin' to be seen in it but water.

Isabel.—Perhaps you'll like this better. Here are some ruins of ancient Greece.

Aunt N.—O la! don't put it down here on my new gownd if it's greasy. Sho! you're jest makin' game; that un is as clean lookin' as the best of 'em. My! but it must have been a shacklin' man that owned that place. It's all gone to rack. I think I'd hev spent the money it took for gettin' the picter took to put it in a leetle better repair.

Isabel.—Ruins are not to my taste either, Auntie. Ah! here's a gem—these Corinthian pillars.

Aunt N.—Ruther hard pillers, I should say; look more like posts. They're stood up, too. I s'pose that's so as to give a good view of 'em. Made for giants, by the size of 'em. Now, that picter's what I call interestin'. Got any more?

Isabel.—This snow scene, Aunt Nancy, is thought to be fine.

Aunt N.—Now, I call that real purty. I allers did set store by a good snow-storm. Sort of chirks one up to hear the bells a-jinglin'. Many a sleighin'-party I went to when I was a gal, and good times we had a-dancin' and a-eatin' the good suppers that was got up. The picter makes me think of it all, and I like it fust-rate. [*Taking up another.*] O, here's a dear little baby. How pert and sassy he looks! Jest for all the world like Sal Smith's little Joe, only Joe's got a squint like in one eye and his nose turns up a leetle.

Isabel.—Not very complimentary to Greuze's Infant Cherub. What do you think of this?

Aunt N. (*scrutinizing it closely and reading aloud the title*).—"Execution of Mary Stuart." Well, there! that's the first I knowed she was dead. Executed, too! I wonder what she'd been and done? Queer I hadn't heerd of it afore. She was old Stuart's daughter, you know, Isabel, down there at Tubbsville.

Isabel.—Oh, you're altogether mistaken, Aunt Nancy. This was a beautiful young queen, who perished centuries ago.

Aunt N.—Well, I am glad to hear it. That is, I'm glad it's not the gal I knowed, she allers seemed so peaceable like.

Isabel.—Here are two pretty little companion-pieces, "Demanding Toll" and "Passing Free." You'll under-stand them at a glance.

Aunt N.—I see a gal and a feller standin' on a bridge, but I don't see no toll-gate. O now I know [*laughing*], them's lovyers. Many a time was I asked to "pay toll" when I was young and handsome, but that was so long ago that I'd e'en a'most forgot what the sayin' meant. Passin' free, is she? Well, she'll come back agin if he coaxes her up a leetle. It's nateral to fight shy for a leetle spell, but they don't ginerally hold out long. I'd have them framed and hung up.

Isabel.—Perhaps I will sometime, but I hear the lunch-bell, so let us put them away and finish looking at them some other time.

Aunt N.—Jest as you say, Isabel. I like your picters fust-rate. When you come to visit me I'll show you my chromios. I got most of them at the tea-store down to Tubbsville, and they're what I consider handsome.

[*Exit.*]

L. J. AND E. C. ROOK.

BRAVE BOSTON BOYS.

CHARACTERS.

GOVERNOR GATES.   HIS SECRETARY.   FOUR BOYS.

SCENE.—*Four boys standing in front of a table at which Secretary is writing. Enter Governor Gates. Takes seat beside table.*

Governor.—Mr. Secretary, what is our business with these lads?

Secretary.—They have come to see your Excellency upon a matter which they had best speak of themselves.

Governor.—Well, boys, what is your errand?

First Boy.—We are here, sir, to complain of what your soldiers have done to us. They have outraged—

Governor.—What! Have your fathers been teaching you rebellion and sent you here to show it?

First Boy.—Nobody sent us, sir; but if our fathers hate oppression, so do we, and we have come to you for redress.

Governor.—Ha, ha! a pretty piece of impudence, I declare. Well, my lad [*turns to third boy*], you seem warlike enough to whip a whole company of my red-coats. What say you?

Third Boy.—If I were a man, sir, I would teach them better manners.

Governor.—What have the soldiers done to you?

First Boy.—They have torn down our snow hills and broken our skating ponds and—

Governor.—That is provoking; but even soldiers must have their frolic.

Fourth Boy.—We could have excused one offense, but that did not satisfy them.

Governor.—Well, the loss of a day's coasting is not hard

to bear. Ah, my boys, you follow the example of your elders and make a pretext for rebellion out of a trifle. The spirit is in you all.

First Boy.—Then, sir, we have caught it from our English grandfathers, if our history books speak the truth.

Governor (to Secretary).—What youthful wiseacre have we here? But [*to boys*] to the purpose. Have you complained to the officers of the troops, my boys?

Second Boy.—John [*indicating first boy*] and I went to the General, sir, and others spoke to the Captain, but they laughed at us and called us little rebels—

Third Boy.—And told us to help ourselves if we could.

First Boy.—After this we met at school, sir, and our companions chose us four to come to you. We have never troubled your troops, but they will not allow us to enjoy our sports, and harass us as if we had no rights in our own city.

Governor.—If this is all you learn at your schools, my boys, they had better be closed, for you will one day suffer a greater harm than the loss of an ice pond for such words.

First Boy.—But, sir, if a company of American soldiers—

Governor.—Be very careful, my lad; such words are dangerous!

First Boy.— —of Indians, or French, should break through the walls of your forts and tear them down, would you not feel, sir, that you had been abused and injured enough to make you turn upon them and punish them? We cannot fight our own battles yet, and for that reason alone we ask your interference with these insolent soldiers.

General (to Secretary).—The very children here draw in a love of liberty with the air they breathe. [*Turning to boys.*] Now, tell me, boys, you have all heard of **King** George of England?

All.—Yes, sir.

Governor.—And of the Parliament?

All.—Yes, sir.

Governor.—Well, they are the powers that by divine right make the laws for the nations of which we are all subjects. Now, if our King wanted us to give him our purse for his good and for our own good, should we not be obedient to him?

First Boy.—If he asked it of us as a gift, sir, we might from our patriotism or our generosity, give it to him and a great deal more besides; but if he forced us—

Governor.—What! what! The very babes prattle treason in their cradles. Children must be taught an humbler duty to their King if we would expect loyal men among us.

Fourth Boy.—But, sir—

Governor.—Well, enough of that. When did this happen that you speak of?

First Boy.—It was on the Common, sir. Every winter we build snow hills there to coast our sleds on, and we use the ponds for skating grounds. Last night for the third time the hills were thrown down and the ice cut and broken in the ponds—

Third Boy.—Yes, sir; and when we came, before our school hour this morning, with our skates and sleds we found the Boiled Lobsters—

Governor.—What, lad?

Third Boy.—O, that is what the townspeople call the red-coats, sir. We found them standing over our ground with their muskets in their hands, and they insulted us, and threatened to shoot us if we mended our hills.

Governor.—And what did you do?

Third Boy.—We built up another hill before school, in spite of them, and then we resolved to speak to you, sir, when we were dismissed.

Governor (*to Secretary*).—This is the stuff to make armies of.

Secretary.—It looks, your Excellency, as if it were likely to form an army before many years pass.

First Boy.—If we were old enough, sir—

Governor.—Well, my brave lads, I like your spirit; but you must learn to utter more temperate words.

All.—But, sir—

Governor.—Go now and rest assured if my troops trouble you again they shall suffer punishment for it. [*Governor rises and starts to follow boys to the door. Suddenly he exclaims:*] Hark! are there not drums sounding outside?

First Boy (*who has already reached window or door looking out*).—Yes! Come, boys, the British are out with their muskets and drums, and the crowd is pelting them with snow-balls. Bravo, Dick! See, he struck the Corporal's hat off! They're fighting! Come, we shall miss it! [*Boys run out, shouting.*]

Governor (*turning to Secretary*).—This populace is as fearless as the sea. No barrier can subdue it. What an omen there seems for us in its roar! Quick! send for my arms. I must quell this riot or it will swell to revolution.

[CURTAIN.]

MORRIS HARRISON.

JUSTICE.

CHARACTERS.

Mr. Harding,	Mr. Martin.
Francis Harding,	Mrs. Martin.
a boy of seventeen.	Harry Martin.
Mr. Brooks, a lawyer.	Alice Martin.

Scene I.

Mr. Harding's office. Mr. H. and Mr. Brooks seated at a table, writing. Enter Francis, throwing down his books and seating himself by the table.

Francis.—Father, Harry Martin is going to leave the Academy. He says his father has lost so much by the contract to put up those houses of yours on State Street, that he will have to sell his property, and Harry is going to leave school and go in an office.

Mr. Harding.—Yes, I believe that has been a losing business for Martin. It was very unfortunate for him.

Francis.—But, father, could you not allow him some share of your profits on the work ?

Mr. Harding (somewhat sternly).—My son, you do not understand business transactions. When you are a few years older, I hope you may have more wisdom. When the contract was made neither of us knew that the price of labor would advance so much. Had it become cheaper, the loss would have been mine. Such risks must always be taken in business.

Francis (hesitatingly).—Father ?

Mr. Harding (impatiently).—Well.

Francis.—I heard you and Mr. Brooks talking last evening about that new railroad running across Mr. Martin's lot. I don't believe he knows anything about it, you told me not to mention it. It will make his land so much more valuable, that if he were to sell that part, don't you think he could keep his house?

Mr. Harding.—Yes, if he were not obliged to sell at once, and could keep it until the railroad were an assured thing.

Francis.—The road will surely run through his land, Mr. Brooks says it will have to. [*Rising and standing before Mr. H.*] Father, won't you, to please me, buy this property and save Mr. Martin from becoming a bankrupt?

Mr. Harding.—If it is offered for sale I shall probably buy it. And now, I have some business with Mr. Brooks.

Francis.—Oh, thank you, father. Harry will be so pleased if he can keep on with his studies. [*Taking cap and books, leaves the room.*]

Mr. Harding (*turning to Mr. Brooks*).—I fear that boy will never make a business man. If I buy the property I shall pay only what it is worth now, without any reference to the railroad.

Mr. Brooks.—Certainly, sir; what sort of a paradise would we have on this earth if business men acted on the principle of the Golden Rule?

Mr. Harding.—There is not a man in the city that would do differently, and yet I dread that boy's opinion of what he will consider a mean act.

[Curtain.]

Scene II.

Same room as before. Mr. Brooks alone, seated, reading a paper. Enter Francis, who must be dressed to look older than in last scene, with gloves, cane, and high hat.

Francis.—Good-morning, Mr. Brooks.

Mr. Brooks (*rising.*)—Good-morning, sir; allow me, if not too late, to offer my congratulations on your having attained your majority. I had no opportunity of doing so yesterday. [*Handing F. a chair.*]

Francis.—Thank you, Mr. Brooks. I have called to inquire about some business matters. I have been anxiously looking forward to the time when I would have control of my property.

Mr. Brooks.—You have a large income; I had supposed that was amply sufficient for you. I hope you do not intend taking up any of the capital. I trust you will consult me before you invest it in any new speculation. As you know, your father wished me to be your legal adviser, as I had always been his.

Francis.—I do intend using my capital, and I have no doubt you will consider it a very unwise investment.

Mr. Brooks.—What do you wish to do with it?

Francis.—In what I shall do, I do not cast any reflections on my father's actions. He simply did what many others would have done.

Mr. Brooks.—You have not told me yet what you are going to do.

Francis.—I am going to pay Mr. Martin the balance due him on the land father bought of him about four years ago.

Mr. Brooks.—Wh–at? I never heard of such insanity! Why, that land is worth fifty thousand dollars. Do you intend giving him that?

Francis.—What did he receive for it?

Mr. Brooks.—Five thousand.

Francis.—Now, will you tell me what you honestly believe it would have been worth had it been generally known that the railroad would pass through?

Mr. Brooks.—Well, I suppose it might have brought twenty thousand.

Francis.—Then I shall pay Mr. Martin the fifteen thou sand dollars.

Mr. Brooks.—I can never consent to your using your money for any such Quixotic notion. He sold it and was glad to get rid of it.

Francis.—That is no reason he should not have what is rightfully his. I shall be obliged to act without your consent, for I have intended doing it just as soon as the money was in my possession. [*Rising.*]

[CURTAIN.]

SCENE III.

Sitting-room, poorly furnished. Mr. Martin reclining in a chair supported by pillows. Mrs. Martin and Alice sewing.

(*Enter Harry, who throws himself in a chair with an air of weariness.*)

Mrs. Martin.—Well, my son, what fortune to-day?

Harry.—Oh, the same old story. Clerks are being discharged every day instead of employed. There seems to be no work in the city for me.

Mr. Martin.—Do not despair, Harry. There must be a place in the world for everybody.

Harry.—Then my niche must be in such an obscure corner that I cannot discover it.

Alice.—I shall not wait any longer. I will write this evening and accept the position Mrs. Cook has offered me.

Mrs. Martin.—Oh, Alice! how can I spare you to go so far from us, and your father so ill?

Mr. Martin.—Things certainly look very dark for us. If I could regain my strength it would be all right, but with money gone and health gone, it is a poor prospect for the winter.

(*Knock at the door. Alice admits Francis. Mrs. Martin places a chair. Francis says "Good-evening," shaking hands with Harry.*)

Harry.—We have not seen you for a long time.

Francis.—No; after father's death I was away with mother for nearly two years. I am sorry to see you are an invalid, Mr. Martin.

Mr. Martin.—I trust I shall not be so long.

Francis.—I have called this evening to speak about that property on Front Street you sold father. Did you know at that time that its value was likely to be so much increased?

Mr. Martin.—No; certainly I did not, or I shouldn't have sold it for the price I did.

Harry.—Father blames himself for being so short-sighted as not to have seen further into the future. I think his poor health is due to his worrying over that affair.

Mr. Martin.—Yes, yes, had I only known the railroad would soon cross the land, I could have saved myself from ruin and been to-day a prosperous man. Well! [*sighing*] it can't be helped now.

Francis.—No, Mr. Martin, the last few years of anxiety and trouble you have passed through cannot be recalled; but I trust that a simple act of justice may render the outlook for the future more cheerful. I felt, when I was but a boy, that it was not just for one to profit by another's mistake.

Mr. Martin.—I blame no one, Francis. I should have inquired more carefully into the matter.

Francis.—Well, Mr. Martin, we will not ask who was to blame. As father bought the land, I wish you to have the balance due on what you would have considered a fair value for it. Here is my check for fifteen thousand lollars that you can use at any time. [*Holding a check toward him.*]

(*Mr. Martin leans forward, looking at Francis in surprise.*)

Mr. Martin.—Why! I—I do not understand you.

Francis.—It is simply this, sir, that I wish to pay you for your land that is now in my possession. [*Putting the check in Mr. Martin's hand.*]

Mr. Martin (*looking at the check*).—But, Francis, I cannot accept this. You do not owe me anything.

Francis.—Perhaps not, Mr. Martin, from a legal standpoint, but by my standard of conscience I do. I could never be happy, feeling that I was enjoying what rightfully belonged to another.

(*Mr. Martin leans back in his chair and covers his face with his hands.*)

Mrs. Martin (*coming to Mr. Martin's side*).—I would that all business men acted on the same principle. This is a noble and generous act, for which I hope you may be amply rewarded.

Francis.—Do not look upon it in the light of a gift. It is your own money, though rather late in coming to you.

Mr. Martin (*sitting up*).—It is an unselfish deed and one worthy of you. My future life will show my gratitude better than I can now express it.

Harry.—My dear friend [*taking the hand of Francis*], I believe you have saved my father's life. This anxiety was killing him.

Alice.—Let me thank you for the load of care you have lifted from the heart of my dear father and mother. I was beginning to doubt whether any one, nowadays, lived by the Golden Rule, but you have clearly proven to-night that it still has force.

[CURTAIN.]

ELLA H. CLEMENT.

A CHRISTMAS EVE ADVENTURE.

CHARACTERS.

SANTA CLAUS.	NELLIE,	
MRS. SANTA CLAUS.	HARRY,	
MR. BENTLY.	FIRST FAIRY,	} Little children.
MRS. BENTLY.	SECOND FAIRY,	
A YOUNG LADY.	THIRD FAIRY,	
THREE SHEPHERDS.	SEVERAL ADULTS AND CHILDREN.	

SCENE I.

A sitting-room nicely furnished. A little boy and girl seated in rocking-chairs.

Nellie.—Harry, don't you wish there were fairies nowadays?

Harry.—Why, Nellie, what a funny question! What could the fairies do?

Nellie.—Help us go to see Santa Claus, to be sure.

Harry.—Do you think they could do that?

Nellie.—Of course they could. Didn't they do all sorts of wonderful things in my new book, "The Enchanted Princess."

Harry.—Well then, I wish they would help us, for I do want to see Santa Claus. I am afraid he won't know all the things I want.

Nellie.—Do you think we could walk to his house to-morrow?

Harry.—Walk! I guess not. He lives up in the moon.

Nellie.—Oh! Then the man in the moon is Santa Claus?

Harry.—H'm, I—suppose—so. I never heard of but one man up there.

Nellie.—If that's where he lives, we can't get there. There is no use in thinking about it.

Harry.—Oh dear. What shall we do with ourselves?

Nellie.—Mamma said I must not come in her room, and Mary told me to run out of the kitchen and not be after botherin' her.

Harry.—Yes, and I was going in the library, when papa came to the door and told me I was not on any account to go in that room.

Nellie (yawning).—Everybody has something to do but us. I am so sleepy, I wish it was bedtime.

Harry.—I am sleepy, too. I'll tell you what to do, Nellie; let's take a nap till supper-time.

Nellie.—Well, suppose we do, then we won't be bothering anybody. Shut your eyes, and I'll shut mine.

(*Both lean back in their chairs and close their eyes.*)

[CURTAIN.]

SCENE II.

Same room. Children sleeping.

Mrs. Bently (comes in and looks at children).—Well, the little darlings are tired out and have gone sound asleep. I will not disturb them. [*Takes her work-basket from the table and goes out.*]

(*Enter three little girls dressed in white to represent fairies, each carrying a wand with a bright ribbon twisted around it. There should be several small bells sewed on the ribbon so that they will ring when the wands are moved.*)

First Fairy.—Shall we aid these children?

Second Fairy.—Did they not wish for our presence?

Third Fairy.—And have we not left our dance on the velvet sward, by the side of the rippling brook, where the flowers were nodding and bending to us, to come to this cold land? Ugh! I'm shivering now.

First Fairy.—Then let us at once to work. [*Goes to the children, waves her wand over them three times.*]

O children dear,
    In your dreams so bright,
May you swiftly speed,
    Through the frosty night,
To the palace fair,
That is built in air,
Where dwelleth in state,
So noble and great,
The good Kris-Kingle,
For whom our merry bells jingle.
    (*All tinkle their bells.*)

Second Fairy (*waving her wand*).—
    Tinkle, tinkle, merry bells,
    By flowery meads and fairy dells,
    Guide these children on their way
    To the place where fairies stay.

Third Fairy (*waving her wand*).—
    There you may see the sly old elf,
    The good St. Nicholas himself.
    (*All tinkle their bells and say in concert,*)
    Tinkle, tinkle, merry bells,
    By flowery meads and fairy dells.
        [CURTAIN.]

SCENE III.

Home of Santa Claus. A profusion of toys scattered about on tables, chairs, and floor. Mrs Santa Claus, with cap and spectacles on, dressing a large doll. A timid knock at the door.

Mrs. S. C. (*looking up*).—Come in.

(*Enter Nellie and Harry dressed same as last scene.*)

Mrs. S. C. (*in great surprise*).—Why, bless my heart!
Where did you two tots come from? [*Kissing each of*

them.] It does my eyes good to look at a child once more. I haven't seen one since Nick and I moved up here. But dear me, what did you come for?

Harry.—Please ma'am, we want to see Santa Claus.

Mrs. S. C.—He isn't at home now, but he soon will be. He has just run over to China. But sit right down. [*Giving each a chair. The children gaze in admiration at the toys scattered about.*]

Nellie.—Are you Mrs. Santa Claus?

Mrs. S. C.—Yes, I am Mrs. Santa Claus.

Harry.—Why, I never knew there was one before.

Nellie (scornfully).—Who did you s'pose dressed all the dolls? Do you think Santa Claus can sew?

Mrs. S. C. (nodding).—It does me good to see you. But tell me, my dears, how you got here?

Harry.—The fairies brought us.

Nellie (looking intently at the doll Mrs. S. C. is dressing). —Mrs. Santa Claus, do you think your husband is going to bring that doll to our house?

Mrs. S. C.—Now, I shouldn't wonder if it was intended for a little girl that looks like you.

Nellie (clapping her hands).—O my, s'pose it is.

(*A stamping and ringing of sleigh-bells heard outside. Santa Claus rushes in. He should be stout, with a long, white beard. A large basket or pack strapped on his back.*)

Santa Claus (sees the children and starts back).—Dear me! Bless my soul! Where did you come from?

Mrs. S. C.—They came to see you on important business.

Santa Claus —Ha! ha! ha! What business can two children have with Santa Claus?

Harry.—Please, Mr. Santa Claus, we were afraid you would not know just what we want for Christmas.

Nellie.—And we thought it would be nicer to come and tell you.

Santa Claus.—Yes, yes, to be sure; so it is, so it is. [*Opening a large account-book.*] Let me see—what are your names? [*Turning the pages of the book.*]

Harry.—Harry and Nellie Bently, sir.

Santa Claus.—Yes, yes, to be sure. Now, what is it you want? [*Taking a pen and writing.*]

Nellie.—A big wax doll and—and a box of cream chocolate candy.

Santa Claus.—Ahem! Candy is a bad thing for little girls. And you, sir? [*Turning to Harry.*]

Harry.—A pair of skates, and a ball, and a Chatterbox, and a new sled, and—

Nellie.—If you please, sir, I'd like a fairy book, and a music-box.

Santa Claus.—Yes, yes, to be sure, you shall have them. Is that all?

Both Children.—Yes, sir.

(*Stamping and sleigh-bells ringing outside.*)

Santa Claus (*turning to Mrs. S. C. and taking the basket from his shoulders*).—My dear, will you have this basket filled with dolls by the time I come back? I hear the rein- deer prancing and pawing out there, so I must be off. I am going to Norway, and can drop these children in the United States, as I go along.

Mrs. S. C.—Well, if they are going with you they must be well bundled up, for it will not be a fairy barge, such as they came in.

Santa Claus.—Yes, to be sure. [*He wraps a buffalo robe around each. Mrs. Santa Claus kisses them and says good- bye. Santa Claus carries them out. A loud ringing of bells and cracking of whips.*]

[CURTAIN.]

Scene IV.

The room brilliantly lighted. A Christmas tree handsomely trimmed, which may be hidden during the previous part of the entertainment by a curtain. Several adults and children seated in the room. Each child should have one or more toys. Nellie and Harry in the foreground, with the different articles for which they had asked Santa Claus, about them. Mr. and Mrs. Bently standing by the tree.

Mr. Bently.—Friends, I believe the presents have all been distributed. I trust no one has been forgotten.

Mrs. Bently (taking up a package).—Here is something you have overlooked.

Mr. Bently.—It is marked for Miss Nellie Bently.

Nellie (takes it and opens it).—Oh ! A box of cream chocolates. [*Excitedly.*] Now, papa, mamma, don't you believe that we really went to see Santa Claus? For we have every single thing we asked him for.

Mrs. Bently.—I think you had a very pleasant dream, seated in the big rocking-chair.

Harry.—Well, we did see him, and Mrs. Santa Claus too, didn't we Nellie?

Nellie (nodding her head emphatically).—Yes, we did.

Mr. Bently.—Let them believe in it; such a harmless superstition can do them no injury. They will begin to doubt soon enough. I believe in letting children be children as long as possible. And now we will have some music, after that perhaps we may have some visitors.

(Music, "Hark! the Herald Angels Sing," or anything appropriate to Christmas. During this piece three men or large boys enter, dressed as shepherds, with shepherds' crooks. They go to the front, and when the music ceases they recite together, or each may recite to a period :)

" When Bethlehem's plains were transfigured with light,
    And the shepherds stood gazing below,
They saw in the heavens above them a sight
    That kindled their hearts to a glow.
On the edge of a cloud stood the Angel of God,
    With legions cherubic attended,
While voices unnumbered, both near and abroad,
    In melodious chorus were blended.
' I bring,' said the Angel, on wings of love flying,
    ' Joy ! joy ! to this desolate sod ;
In Bethlehem's manger a Saviour is lying
    Who is Christ, the Incarnate of God !'
Then the cherubic legions praised God in full chorus,
And this was the song that rang out on the air,

        (*To be sung by the entire company :*)

        Gloria Deo in Excelsis,
        Peace on earth, good will to men."

  (*The shepherds step back, and a young lady goes to front of*
stage and recites :)

  " The Arab now pitches his tent on the plain
    Where the shepherds heard angels once sing,
And the Mussulman's war-steed now crunches his grain
    In the manger that cradled our King !
But the warm, living faith and the heart's pure devotion
    The angels enkindled in bosoms of old,
Have swept the wide world, and from ocean to ocean,
    Till millions rejoice when the story is told.
And the Saviour no more is a babe in the manger,
    But a conquering hero, all mighty to save,
To the helpless a refuge, a friend to the stranger,
    E'en wielding a sceptre o'er death and the grave.

Let us take up the song, then, and join the grand chorus,
As sung to the shepherds on Bethlehem's plains;
The same Christ is ours, the same heaven o'er us,
And angels are waiting to join the glad strain.

(*To be sung by the company:*)

Gloria in Excelsis,
Peace on earth, good will to men."

[Curtain.]

ELLA H. CLEMENT.

DOUBLE PLAY.

CHARACTERS.

MR. JUDSON, a millionaire from Michigan, very delicate.
TOM CARMINE, a young artist looking for a model.
FRITZ OPPELHEIMER, a German who has had experience.
MIKE O'LEARY, an Irish grocery store clerk.

SCENE.—*Parlor in Mrs. Mulberry's boarding house. Lounge at right, table in centre, on which are newspapers. One chair at right and two at left. Mr. Judson discovered lying on lounge asleep, with shawl thrown over him. Enter Tom Carmine, wearing Tam O'Shanter cap, Norfolk jacket, and negligé tie. Contemplates Mr. Judson's sleeping form.*

Tom.—What on earth does that fellow want lying about the parlor in that fashion, I'd like to know? Why don't he go to his room and sleep? A nice idea, that, to make a chamber out of the drawing room! And I expect visitors, too—any number of them—in answer to my advertisement for a model. Mrs. Mulberry objects to my having them tramp over her new stair carpets up to the fourth floor, so I have to receive them here instead of in my sky-parlor studio. What a jolly model this old fellow would make!

He's got just the cadaverous, worn expression I want, but of course, he wouldn't consent to sit. Mrs. Mulberry tells me he's immensely wealthy. Don't know how to spend his income, and is looking for a long-lost nephew with whom to share it. Of course he wouldn't sit. I wish he'd get up and go, though. Well, when the consumptive models begin to come in he won't stop long; their coughing will disturb his slumbers. [*Going to table and taking up a paper, reads:*] " WANTED—A thin, hollow-cheeked man as a model, by an artist, who is about to paint a picture of ' Tantalus in Hades.' Call at 76 Boffin's Bower, between eleven and twelve." There, that's my advertisement. Rather neat, I think. As I view it, Tantalus must have been very much emaciated after his efforts to get a mouthful of water had continued for some time, and so I shall picture him. I want as a model, a man dying of consumption, with his skin drawn tightly over the cheek-bones, his cheeks two deep holes, his eyes sunken, his complexion pale and sallow. How well that sleeper there would answer my purpose! By Jove! I think I'll make a sketch of his face as he sleeps. Where's my sketch-book? [*Feels in his pockets.*] Up stairs, of course. Well, it won't take me long to get it. [*Exit Tom, L.*]

(*As he goes out, Mike O'Leary peeps in at R. Then steps cautiously in on tiptoe.*)

Mike.—Whist, now! And phat's this I'm doin'? Sure, I might be arristed for burgulary and clapped into a dungeon cell fur false pretinses. Mike O'Leary, me boy, you've no right here, at all at all, and it's a coward yez are or yez wouldn't run away loike that from a purty face and a tidy waist—the wan wantin' to be kissed by you and the ither imbraced. Bad cess to the gurl wid her flattery! It was at the back gate I called jist now to take Mrs. Mulberry's

ordthers fur the corner grocery, whin the little colleen in
vited me in, and "It's a model ye are," sez she. "Go way
wid yez!" sez I ; "it's yerself as is the pink of perfection,"
sez I. Wid that I was about to put me arrum about her,
whin she pointed to this door. "It's a Tantalus yez would
be," sez she. "Tantalizin' ye?" sez I. "Niver a bit of
it, but a thrue admirer of your rosy cheeks and bright
eyes," sez I, and wid that I was about to kiss her. Then
I heard futshtips a comin' and I—well, here I am, and
phat I'm here fur I don't know! Sure, the ould man's a
wakin' up there, and I'm blissed if I know how to explain
me prisence here, at all at all.

(*Mr. Judson opens his eyes, looks about sleepily, catches
sight of Mike, and sits up on lounge.*)

Mr. Judson.—Ah! you called to see me, I suppose.

Mike.—I did, sir! [*Aside.*] I must get out of this some
way or other ; and sure, since I'm here I've called to see
him.

Mr. Judson.—I hope you will excuse the manner of my
reception of you. The fact is, I was very weary, and I
fell asleep almost before I knew it. Have you been waiting
long?

Mike.—Not very long, sir.

Mr. Judson.—And you came in answer to my advertisement, I suppose.

Mike (aside).—Phat luck, to be sure! [*Aloud.*] I did
that, sir ; yes, sir. In answer to your advertisement, sir.

Mr. Judson.—Won't you sit down?

Mike (seating himself on chair by lounge).—Thank ye,
sir!

Mr. Judson.—I may as well explain to you that my sister came east from Michigan twenty five years ago, and
here married a poor man. Who or what he was I don't

know. I never heard his name. She and my father had a quarrel, and after her departure we received no letter or message from her. A mutual friend who met her here years afterward, informed us she was married and had a son. That son I now want to find. Therefore I advertised for information concerning Margaret Judson or her child. What do you know of either of them?

Mike.—Niver a word, sir !

(*Enter Tom Carmine, L., portfolio in hand.*)

Mr. Judson.—But I thought you said you came in answer to the advertisement; and yet when I ask you what you know, you can tell me nothing.

Tom (*interposing*).—Pardon me, sir; but it is probably my advertisement to which this young man has responded. I advertised for a model.

Mike (*aside*).—Shure it's thrue the fairies are good to the Irish. [*Aloud.*] That's it, sir; I'm a model, sir; at least I've been towld so, sir.

Tom.—But I advertised for a thin, delicate looking man. Surely you don't mean to say you answer that description!

Mike.—Ah sir, it's puffed up wid pride I am, sir, to be honored by the likes o' you, sir. Ordinarily, sir, I'm that thin that ye can't see me wid a microschope whin I stand sideways. Faith, whin the living skiliton was too sick to appear at the Dime Museum, I tuck his place as a substhitute, and I was that thin, sir, that siventeen ladies fell in love wid me, while wan hunthred and twinty siven bought me fortygraph the first day I was on exhibition.

(*Knock at door, L.*)

Mr. Judson and Tom (*in chorus*).—Come in !

(*Enter Fritz Oppelheimer.*)

Mr. Judson.—You wish to see me ?

Tom.—You have called in answer to—

Fritz.—Yah! das is recht. I haf galled in anzer to dot nodis by de baber.

Mr. Judson.—As I said, you wish to give me some infor- mation about my nephew—my sister's child—you have—

Mike.—It's a model he is, to be sure. Begorra, we are both practisin' the same profession.

Tom.—Did you wish to see the artist?

Fritz.—Yah! It vhas de ardisd I to see vhas vantin. I haf krade sugcess as a model. I haf bosed for ardists in Perlin, Vienna, Paris, efferywhere. For twendy five years I have bosed here in dis ciddy. I haf efferyding peen!— varrior, loffer, Gubid, efferyding!

Mike.—Cupid is it! Faith, a foine bouncin' Cupid wud you make! Have yez iver thried Apollo of the Velvet Ear?

Tom.—Excuse me, sir; but I hope you won't interfere with this gentleman.

Fritz.—Sho! I mind not what he says. He was Irish. He vill haf his laedle choke. May I imbose a story ubon you? Eh! Vell, all ride! It vas shord. Shall ve sid town?

Tom.—Certainly. [*Places chair. All sit.*]

Mr. Judson.—I hope my presence is not an intrusion, sir.

Tom.—O not at all. Take a chair and hear our friend— I beg pardon, sir; your name is—

Fritz.—Fritz Oppelheimer. [*Mr. Judson takes chair.*]

Tom.—Well, Fritz, we're listening.

Fritz.—Yah, das in recht. Fifteen years ako I vas haf my live safed by von Irish shentleman. Peesiness vas ferry pad. I vas ferry boor. I say, Fritz, old poy, you're live vas no goot. You pedder vas gone died.

Mike.—Shure, it 'ud been only one Dootchmon the less,

and that's shmall account! [*Picks up Tom's portfolio and examines it.*]

Fritz.—Town py de tocks I vas valkin', ven all of a suddin I dakes a notion I vill end myselluf. De nide vas tark—so tark you noddings can see almost. Vell! I make gvick vork. Sblash! indo de vader I ko. O zo gold it vas I soon vish mysselluf oud again. I sdruggle and sdruggle, but no koot! All krows tarker und tarker. My het she hums und hums und hums. Pride lides tance pefore mine eyes; den I no more knows. I dinks I vas ded, meppe; pud no, I vas all ride afder all. It vas an Irish shentleman vot safed me. He hert my sblash and he shumped in afder me. Vell, I neffer forgod dot Irishman for dot. It vas so prave, so goot.

Tom.—How odd! Why, do you know, Fritz, my father was an Irish gentleman, and he once saved the life of a German in just the way you describe. He was in hard luck at the time, and was employed as private watchman down along the wharves.

Fritz.—Ish dot so? My resguer vas a brivate vatchman doo.

Tom.—What was his name?

Fritz.—Dom Garmine.

Tom.—Then it was my father, Tom Carmine; I am named for him.

Fritz (in amazement).—Ish dot so! And you vas his son. Vell I vas zo klat to meed you. I rememper you ven you vas so high. And vere is your fader now? [*Shake hands.*]

Tom.—Dead and gone, Fritz.

Fritz.—Und your mudder? O she vas sooch a nice laty. She koom from de Vest, eh?

Tom.—Yes. She came from Michigan. She too is dead.

Mr. Judson.—She came from Michigan, did you say?

Tom.—I did, yes sir. Did you know her?

Mr. Judson.—What was her name?

Tom.—Carmine, sir, Mrs. Carmine!

Mr. Judson.—Yes, but her maiden name? [*Excitedly.*] What was her name before she was married?

Tom.—Her name was Judson, sir! Margaret Judson.

Mr. Judson (*still more excitedly*).—You don't mean it? You're joking! Surely, you are not the son of Margaret Judson?

(*Mike draws paper with seal upon it from portfolio of sketches which he is still looking over, unfolds it, and reads attentively.*)

Tom.—I'm no one else, sir. But why do you wish to know? Was she a friend of yours, sir?

Mr. Judson.—She was my sister, sir; and if you are her son, you must be my nephew; and if you are my nephew, you are—

Tom.—Heir to your fortune, eh, uncle? Well, Uncle Judson, look no further. The long lost is found. [*Aside.*] The very idea! Why, I hadn't the slightest notion that this gentleman was my mother's brother.

Mr. Judson.—Yes, yes, my boy. But where are your proofs that you are my nephew? Your mere statement goes for very little, you know. Any one could say that.

Mike.—Sure, here are his proofs, sir. Phat more do yez want thin a marridge certificate, and here it is. [*Producing paper with seal. Mr. Judson takes it eagerly and reads*].

Tom.—Yes sir; there you have it.

Mr. Judson.—Well, this certainly seems all right. How strange that I should find the very boy I advertised for right here under the same roof with me! [*Grasps Tom's and heartily.*] And so you're Margaret's son? Well, my lad, I'm proud of you!

Tom.—Thank you, uncle. I'm sure I'm proud to be your nephew. And wasn't it strange that I should find in you, just what I want for a model for my picture of Tantalus?

Mr. Judson.—What? Do you want to paint me?

Tom.—Well, no; not now, under the circumstances, I guess not. But I did think your face would do. To tell the truth, I've rather decided to make Tantalus a fat man instead of a thin one, and I shall engage Fritz here for the part.

Fritz.—Yah! das is recht.

Mike.—And phat will ye engage me fur? Sure, it was I who established your claim to the title.

Tom.—If I am not mistaken, your name is Mike O'Leary, my man, and your place is behind the counter at the corner grocery. What you are doing in Mrs. Mulberry's parlor I don't exactly know, but if you value your—

Mike.—All right, sir; I'm going, sir. [*Aside.*] Sure, I was afraid I'd be arristed for burgulary or highway robbery or something of that sort.

Tom.—And should you meet any people coming in answer to one or both of the advertisements, as you appear to have done, you can tell them that their services are not required. We have had a double play.

Mike.—That I will, sir. [*Exit hurriedly.*]

[CURTAIN.]

CHARLES STOKES WAYNE.

THE GHOST OF CROOKED LANE.

CHARACTERS.

DR. DUDLEY GRABALL, old and eccentric.
NED HAMESTRAP, in love with Mattie.
SAMMY SMOOTHWAY, a dandy, also in love with Mattie.
MATTIE GRABALL, the Doctor's lovely daughter.
AUNT CHARITY, housekeeper, cross and nervous.

SCENE.—*A library. Table and chairs in centre. Writing material, a large wooden lancet, and pair of tongs on table. Lounge near left entrance. Flour barrel painted black, with the word leeches on it in white letters, standing near right entrance; barrel to contain two leeches three feet long, made of brown muslin and painted to imitate. Window practical, with white curtain, at rear of table. Door practical, at rear of table. Time, evening. Doctor discovered at table reading book.*

Doctor (*rises*).—This is a very valuable book on the application of the leech, but it is too dark to pursue the subject further. I want more light. [*Lays book on table, goes to L. E. and calls.*] Charity! [*Aside.*] What a stupid, idle, negligent, worthless old woman that is! [*Aloud.*] Charity! I say! I say! I say—! Char-i-ty!

Charity (*from without*).—Well, what is it now? A tireder woman, nor a wuss treated creetur' don't live on this earth. [*Enter L. E.*] What is it now, you impatient mortal? What is it?

Doctor.—Bring me a light; do you hear? A light; I want a light. Don't stand there like an oil derrick, but go!

Charity.—Oh, you can of dynamite! You broke my poor sister's heart, and sent her headlong to an early grave—

Doctor.—Be off, or I'll send you headlong. Be off, I say—

Charity.—Ugh! you wretched man.

[*Exit L. E.*]

Doctor (*resumes seat at table*).—Was ever a man afflicted with such a female snapping turtle? If I did not know that she dotes on Mattie I would get a new housekeeper in the morning. By the way, that reminds me that it is time Mattie is home from singing school.

Charity (*re-enters with lighted candle, which she sets on table*).—There! I wish you'd teach your daughter to keep better hours; it's dark in the lane, and supper's been ready more than an hour. You know for two weeks past there's been queer stories told about somethin' awful prowlin' in the lane. I believe it's Nat Tompkins' sperrit— the fellow you bled in the arm the night he died. They say he buried his money in the—

Doctor.—Stop right there! Do you mean to insinuate that because I bled him in the arm—

(*Enter Mattie, screaming; door to remain open.*)

Charity.—Horror! Horror!

Doctor.—Keep off! Keep off! [*Picks up lancet and flourishes it.*]

Mattie.—Save me! save me! [*Runs to lounge and hides face.*]

Doctor (*goes to lounge*).—Mattie, my child, what's the trouble? Tell your poor old father.

Mattie.—I saw it in the lane. It chased me from the spring house to the door. Oh! oh! oh!

(*Charity screams and kneels beside Mattie.*)

Doctor.—Ha! Where is it? Show it to me! [*To Charity.*] Go shut the door; do you hear? Go, the draught is too strong.

Charity (rising).—Go yourself; I'm afeared.

Mattie (looking up).—Don't you go near the door, father , I am sure it's waiting outside.

Doctor.—I'm afraid of nothing. [*Advancing toward door.*] Show yourself, if you dare! I don't know the meaning of the word fear. [*Stands in front of open door.*]

Mattie.—Father! father!

Charity.—Dudley Graball, you're a temptin' fate!

Doctor (turns, facing Mattie and Charity, with back to door).—I'm ashamed of you.

(*Ghost appears, enveloped in a sheet; remains standing in doorway.*)

(*Mattie and Charity scream and point at door.*)

Doctor (flourishes lancet).—Come, come; if twenty spectres appeared, I'd, I'd—[*Turns to door.*] Oh! Mur-dab! [*Drops lancet, falls on floor, and shouts.*] Take it away! take it away!

(*Ghost vanishes.*)

Charity.—Oh, oh! I'm trimblin' from head to foot. Mattie, dear, it's gone.

Mattie.—Yes, it has disappeared; I never had such a shock in my life. [*Mattie closes the door.*]

Charity.—Oh, child, be careful!

Mattie (shakes Doctor).—Get up, father; it has gone, and the door is shut.

Doctor (rises and looks about cautiously, picks up lancet and examines it).—This lancet bears no stain of blood, yet I ran it through him four times, and then I slipped down. Gone? Yes, I guess it has gone.

Charity.—Come, supper's waitin'; a cup o' tea'll compose your nerves.

Doctor.—Yes, we'll go to supper. Come, Mattie, love, come and refresh yourself. Ham, hominy, and potatoes are good antidotes. A full stomach is a surety against ghosts. Come, pet.

Mattie.—Thanks, father, but we had a lunch at singing school, and I am not a bit hungry. I'll sit here while you and Aunt Charity go down.

Charity.—Poor child; just like her mother; no appetite.

Doctor.—Well, let us go. Don't stand there winking at the ceiling. You're the most timid old maid I ever saw. I say, come!

(*Exit Doctor and Charity, L. E. Light knock at door.*)

Mattie (goes to door).—Who's there?

Hamestrap.—'Tis I; let me in, Mattie.

Mattie (opens door).—Ned Hamestrap, as I live! For the love of goodness don't make a noise! They have just gone to supper.

Hamestrap (enters).—For the love of you I'd do anything.

Mattie (closes door).—Let us sit on the lounge; we can better hear them there. I am glad you have come, but I fear the case is hopeless. You know father will not allow me to have any company at all; you have been sent off five times already.

Hamestrap.—I can but try. I will put the question to the Doctor this very night. I must know the worst.

Mattie.—It is so strange that father forbids all young men the house.

Hamestrap.—Wretchedly absurd, my dear girl! Horribly shabby and unwise.

Mattie.—Hark! I hear my parent's voice!

Hamestrap (jumping up).—I'd better go.

Doctor (calls).—Mattie!

Mattie.—Sir?

Doctor.—Who are you talking to?

Mattie.—Why, father, dear, n-n-n-never mind. [*To Hamestrap.*] Be still as a mouse.

Doctor.—There must be another spirit up there. Don't be afraid, I'm coming.

(*Hamestrap runs to door.*)

Mattie.—There's no necessity, I'm not a bit scared. Don't come.

Doctor.—Duty calls me; I must.

Hamestrap (*aside*).—It calls me, too. [*Aloud.*] The door's locked! Quick, Mattie, unfasten it or I am caught!

Mattie.—Pull hard, it only sticks.

Doctor.—What's that? Another ghost? Mur-dah!

(*Mattie screams. Doctor enters running. Hamestrap tries to open door.*)

Doctor.—What are you doing here, sir?

Mattie.—He's trying to keep the ghost out.

Hamestrap.—I came just in time.

Doctor.—You did, eh? Well, I'm obliged to you; but, as I have ordered you out before, it is only necessary for me to say, go! Go, I say! [*Chases Hamestrap around room.*]

Hamestrap (*running*).—One moment. I beg to remain.

(*Enter Charity, who follows and strikes Hamestrap with broom.*)

Doctor.—Not a word. My daughter is too young.

Mattie.—Spare him! Spare him!

Doctor.—Away! out! It's my cash you are after!

(*Hamestrap opens door and exits.*)

Mattie.—That is the most cruel thing you ever did. I never thought you would be so hard hearted as to drive a poor, innocent young man out into the very arms of a hobgoblin. You know the whole village is wild over this strange apparition.

Doctor.—So am I, but I prefer spectres to speculators.
(*Loud knock at door.*)

All (*start*).—Oh!

Mattie.—Be cautious.

Doctor.—I will see who's there.

(*Loud double knock and groan. Mattie and Charity scream.*)

Charity (*takes position near door with broom raised*).— I'm ready, Dudley.

Doctor (*runs to table, takes up lancet*).—Open the door, Charity.

Charity.—Who are you?

Sammy.—It's me, Samuel Smoo-moo-moo-moothway. I want to see the Doctor. M-m-my jaw's breaking.

Mattie.—Sammy's voice, I know it well. Let him in.

Charity (*opening door*).—Come in.

(*Enter Sammy, with head wrapped in large scarf.*)

Sammy.—Oh—!

Charity (*strikes him with broom*).—I thought you were the spook.

Sammy.—D-d-d-d-don't do that again. I am suffering with a toothache in my neck.

Mattie.—Poor fellow. Come take a seat on the lounge.

Sammy (*sits on lounge*).—Thanks! [*Aside.*] Oh, the lovely rosebud! The touch of that hand would scatter the too-too-toothache, even if I had it. [*Removes scarf from head.*] It's much better now.

Doctor (*advances to Sammy with tongs*).—I think we had better remove the tooth; take away the cause and the effect's nowhere.

Sammy.—N-n-n-no you don't. It's the neuralgia. It is in my neck.

Doctor.—Let me examine it.

Sammy.—Keep them nippers away. [*Aside.*] All this to gain the affection of a girl, and she scarcely looks at me. It's t-t-t-too bad.

Doctor.—I see what's the matter; congestion. I'll relieve the pain in three minutes. Just let these ladies steady your head.

Mattie.—Shall I support your head, sir?

Charity.—Of course; take hold of the young man's feet.

Doctor (*goes to barrel and takes out two leeches*).—Hold him tight.

Sammy (*raises head and sees leeches*).—Murder! Take those snakes away! [*He struggles.*] Help! help! W-w-w-watch!

(*Door opens. Ghost appears, groans, and vanishes. All look toward door. Sammy jumps up and rushes out.*)

Doctor.—He's a brave man.

Mattie (*closes door*).—Aunt Charity, we had better go to the dining room.

Doctor.—Yes; get a cup of tea, Mattie. [*Exit Mattie and Charity.*] What have I done to deserve this? I wish I had a boy. [*Sits near table with back toward door.*] I am getting old. I cannot stand this ghost business any longer. [*Takes up book.*] Well, I'll try and resume my studies. Let me see, where did I leave off? Oh, yes: " When the leech takes hold "—yes, that's it. [*Reads.*]

(*Ghost opens door and advances slowly. Touches Doctor on shoulder.*)

Doctor (*looks up and falls on knees*).—Oh! oh, Mercy!

Ghost (*in sepulchral tone*).—Sit in that chair.

Doctor (*rises and sits down*).—Oh, good Mr. Ghost! spare me.

Ghost.—Silence!

Doctor.—Keep away, and I will give you all I possess.

Ghost.—I have but a single favor to ask; grant it, and peace shall be yours, peace shall be mine.

Doctor.—I promise. Name it.

Ghost.—That you permit your daughter to marry Ned Hamestrap.

Sammy (looks in at window).—Aha! [*Disappears.*]

Doctor.—Suppose she won't?

Ghost.—She will.

Doctor.—I promise.

Ghost (retiring slowly).—Farewell!

(*Exit.*)

(*Enter Mattie and Charity.*)

Mattie.—Were you calling us, father?

(*Doctor trembles and points to door. Knock at door.*)

Mattie.—I'm not afraid. [*Opens door.*]

(*Enter Hamestrap.*)

Doctor.—I am so glad to see you.

Hamestrap.—And I am more than delighted to see you all. [*Aside.*] Now's the time. [*Aloud.*] Doctor, I am a man of few words. I love Mattie, and Mattie loves me; have we your permission to wed?

Doctor.—Mattie must answer for herself.

Mattie.—Oh, father!

Doctor.—Come now, Mattie dear; what shall I tell him?

Mattie.—Why, y-e-s—!

(*Hamestrap attempts to embrace Mattie.*)

Doctor.—Hold on! [*Places his arm between them.*] I have overlooked a matter. A horrid ghost has been here—

Hamestrap.—A ghost?

Doctor.—And until I have proof that it will not—

Hamestrap.—I know what you want. Now that I am to be a member of the family, I'll seek out the ghost and send him in to apologize. [*Exit.*]

All.—No, no! [*They move toward L. E.*]

(*Enter Ghost, groaning. Charity brandishes broom, Doctor brandishes lancet. All greatly alarmed.*)

Hamestrap (*throws off sheet*).—It is I!

Doctor.—You rascal!

Mattie (*taking Hamestrap's hand*).—Forgive us, father. It was only a trick of love.

Hamestrap.—Where hearts were trumps. [*Stands with back to door.*] The ghost has gone forever!

(*Enter Sammy, with sheet held before him. He advances softly behind Hamestrap.*)

(*All except Hamestrap point and scream.*)

Hamestrap.—How foolish! It is only the sheet tnat 1 threw off. Besides, I am here.

Charity.—Only look! Oh, look!

Hamestrap (*turns slowly*).—Fire! Fire! Take him off! [*Runs behind Doctor.*]

Sammy.—Enough! I have paid him back. Now I will be his groomsman.

(*All laugh, and take positions. Charity, Mattie, Doctor, Ned, Sammy.*

Doctor (*taking Mattie and Hamestrap by the hand*).— And thus departs the ghost of Crooked Lane!

[CURTAIN.]

GEORGE M. VICKERS.

GOING TO THE DENTIST'S.

CHARACTERS.

JAMES GREEG, a boy of sixteen. ELI GREEG, a boy of fourteen.
DENTIST.

SCENE I.

In a small boarding school study, furnished with a couple of chairs, a small table of books, ordinary lamp, etc. James sitting in the arm chair, his face tied up with a large handkerchief. Eli occupying the other chair beside the table, figuring on his slate.

James (groaning and putting his hand to his face).—It aches awfully, and what a fellow's to do without a mother to doctor him up, I don't know. [*Sobbing.*] This being away from home ain't what it's cracked up to be.

Eli (kindly).—There, don't take on so, brother. It'll stop after a bit. I wouldn't make such a fuss about a tooth.

James (moaning).—Yes, you would, too. I remember about your six year molars. You kept the whole house awake two nights when one ached, and had lots of poultices on and people to sympathize with you.

Eli —Well, I got it out. That's the thing to do.

James.—O it pains dreadfully! Can't you get me a poultice, or something to stop it? Oh—h-oh! [*Pressing both hands to his face and walking around.*]

Eli (putting his arm affectionately about James).—Poor fellow, never mind.

James (moaning).—Huggin's good enough, Eli, but it won't cure toothache. Get me a poultice, laudanum, or something, quick! ugh! oh!

Eli.—I'll go to the kitchen and hunt you a poultice

quicker than you can say Jack Robinson. Hold on, old fellow! [*Running out.*]

James (*throwing himself into the arm chair and holding his jaw with his hand*).—I s'pose nobody ever dies with toothache, but I'd enough rather, than live with it. [*Puts his hand tightly over his mouth, and closes his eyes a moment, moans in a muffled tone.*] Ugh! ugh! Oh! oh! Eli stays an awful while after that poultice. Ugh! ugh! [*In a rather louder, but still smothered voice.*] Eli! Eli! [*Holds his mouth shut and closes his eyes again, moaning.*]

(*Enter Eli with a large, dark, pepper colored plaster on a white cloth.*)

Eli (*aside*).—This ain't like mother makes, but I guess it'll do. Hello, James, tooth any better?

James (*moaning*).—No. Getting worse all the time. Give me your poultice, quick! Ugh!

(*Eli and James together adjust the poultice on the latter's cheek.*)

Eli.—There, now that's like mother put it on, if it ain't the same dose. [*Sneezing.*]

James (*sneezing three or four times*).—Pepper, pepper! ugh! pepper! [*Sneezing several times.*]

Eli.—The nurse said pepper plaster was the very thing. I guess it's too strong. Jerk it off.

(*James sneezes vigorously for a few moments while jerking it off.*)

Eli.—Poor soul. The cure's worse than the disease. Let's have the tooth out.

James.—All right, or I'll be killed with doctoring. [*Sneezing.*]

Eli.—All right! You get it out and I'll pay for it. That's fair.

James (*sneezing and moaning, puts a hat on his head that*

fits illy on account of the handkerchief still around his head).
—Come on to the dentist's.

Eli.—You're a sorry object to go on the street. Some of that plaster's on your face yet.

James (sneezing).—Who cares for looks? Come on.

(*Exit*.)

Eli (taking up his hat and preparing to follow. Aside to the audience).—I expect he'll be afraid to have it out. [*Exit*.]

[CURTAIN FALLS.]

SCENE II.

A dental room. Dentist standing beside a window, near the dental chair, examining and rubbing up his instruments.

Dentist.—These hard times have a bad effect on my trade. Only had four patients yesterday, and two of those went on the books. Rather a bad lookout for a man with a large family to support. [*Bell rings*.] Halloa! There's somebody now.

(*Enter Eli and James as they appeared at the close of former scene, James still holding his face. Eli bows, hat in hand*.)

Dentist.—Good morning, gentlemen, good morning. Lovely day.

Eli.—Good morning. Yes sir, quite pleasant.

Dentist.—Be seated. [*Waving his hand in the direction of vacant chairs. To James*.] Some trouble with the teeth, young man?

James (in a muffled tone, owing to the handkerchief over his mouth).—Got the toothache. [*Sneezing*.]

Dentist.—We'll soon fix that matter. Undo your face and take this chair a moment. [*Indicating the dental chair*.]

James (removing the handkerchief slowly).—Had a pepper

[*sneezing*] plaster on, and it makes me [*sneezing*] sneeze [*Sneezing.*]

Dentist.—Bad things, those pepper plasters. Better have a tooth out at once or filled, when it makes trouble.

James (dolefully).—But it'll hurt.

Dentist (blandly).—Oh, not much.

James (standing on one leg and then the other).—Don't ache much now [*sneezing*], but I may's well let you look at it, I reckon. [*Advancing slowly toward the dental chair.*]

Dentist (invitingly).—Just step up and take a seat. The light's good here.

James (with his hand on the arm of the chair, turning to Eli).—Would you believe it, Eli, the thing's stopped aching?

Eli.—Glad of it. Won't hurt so much to get it jerked.

James (sneezing).—Don't know [*sneezing*] as I'll have it out now.

Dentist.—Sit down and let me take a look, at any rate, that we may decide the case.

(*James occupies the dental chair reluctantly.*)

Dentist.—Lay your head back. [*Adjusting the head with his hand.*] Open your mouth.

James (timidly).—Come here, Eli, and show him the tooth. I don't want him to see the wrong one. [*Sneezes.*]

(*Eli approaches the chair.*)

Dentist.—Open your mouth. I want to see them all. [*Putting his hand on James' chin to assist the mouth in opening.*]

(*James, with his head back, opens his mouth.*)

Dentist (looking at the teeth).—Your teeth are in a bad condition. Two or three need to come out. [*Reaching for an instrument with which to examine them more closely.*]

Eli.—It's a lower one on the right side aches. [*Pointing to it.*]

(James groans, shuts his mouth, sneezes.)

Dentist.—But those decayed molars should be **drawn.**
Let me inspect them more fully.

James.—What's that thing you've got? I ain't ready
for you to pull yet.

Dentist (displaying a small pointed instrument).—Simply
a small instrument with which to examine the condition of
the teeth.

James (groaning).—You won't pull?

Dentist.—No. Open your mouth!

James (lays back his head, sneezing and coughing).—It
makes me sneeze, I tell you, to open my mouth! And
mother won't like it. Give me a drink!

*Dentist (reaching for a tumbler, which sits on the table, and
finds it empty).*—Just hold easy a moment and I'll bring you
water. [*Exit Dentist, tumbler in hand.*]

James (groans).—Raise that window, Eli, to make more
air—quick!

Eli (raises the sash).—Don't get so excited, old fellow.

(James springs to the window and jumps out.)

Eli (looking out).—Zounds! Did you break your neck?

James (calling from without).—I'm right side up with
care. You drink the water and give my compliments to
the dentist.

Eli (looking provoked and puzzled).—Such a baby, to
run for fear he'd get hurt! [*Scratching his head.*] How'll
I manage the dentist? Like enough, he'll want me to turn
patient. Good-bye. [*He swings himself into the window
and disappears just as the Dentist enters.*]

*(Enter Dentist with tumbler of water. As he advances,
notes the absence of James and Eli, and sees the open window;
looks much astonished, almost letting the tumbler fall from his*

hand; recovers, puts it on the table, and rushes to the window, shouting, "Stop thief! stop thief!")

Eli (answering from the distance).—Can't, I've got to catch James.

Dentist (banging down the window and looking about the room).—The most provoking thieves are those of time and patience, and there's no telling what else they took.

[CURTAIN FALLS.]

MRS. S. L. OBERHOLTZER.

THE SEIZURE;

OR,

A SENTIMENTAL MAIDEN'S MISTAKE.

Dramatized from Shandy McGuire, an Irish novel of the early part of the Nineteenth Century.

DRAMATIS PERSONÆ.

CHRISTOPHER JOICE, lieutenant of Revenue Police.

REV. BAXTER CANTWELL, an English clergyman of doubtful character.

SERGEANT AND POLICEMEN (number of policemen may vary from three to twelve).

MISS REBECCA CANTWELL, a maiden of mature years, with youthful aspirations.

MRS. BAXTER CANTWELL, sister-in-law to Rebecca.

MAID.

STAGE PROPERTIES.—Letter, call bell, large valise, stuffed canary, and bird-cage, large dusting brush, small mouth whistle, blunderbuss.

SCENE I.

Room in the Police Barracks. Lieutenant Joice seated at a table with an open letter in his hand.

Lieut. (referring to letter).—Daniel Doogan has this day lodged information that two casks of unpermitted liquor were deposited by James Gallinach, of Lough Devnish, in the cellar of the Rev. Baxter Cantwell. As the smuggled goods are deposited within your district, 1 turn the matter over to you. Signed by the Lieutenant of Police at Stranorlan.

Lieut.—Why, this is most vexatious, absolutely horrible —to search the house for smuggled goods where I have received so much kindness; and a brother Orangeman's too. That brother a magistrate, a minister, and himself the greatest enemy the smuggler ever met upon the bench. If I proceed to the search, I may leave the country at once. The Orangemen of the neighborhood may take my life in revenge for the insult offered their master and chaplain, though he is a villain, and if I don't do my duty I lose my commission. Worse still—there's Miss Cantwell, too; she will never survive it. I am told she is ever speaking of me. I know it. Her attentions to me are unmistakable. I never gave her cause, but what then ?—that don't alter the case; and to bring up a party of Revenue Police to search her brother's house for contraband liquor, ay, that's the mischief of it. Well! [*meditatively*], I'll ring for the Sergeant. [*Rings bell.*] He's a brother and a member of the lodge; perhaps he may devise some plan, for I can't. [*Enter Sergeant.*]

Lieut. Joice.—Read that [*pointing to letter*], and let me hear what you think of it.

Sergeant (*reading*).—To Christopher Joice, Esq., Lieutenant of Revenue Police, Donegal, Dear Sir : Daniel Doogan, etc. [*Reading rapidly the remainder of the letter.*] Very disagreeable. [*Lays letter down again.*]

Lieut. (*emphatically*).—Very !

Sergeant.—But it might be worse, sir.

Lieut.—Worse ! How so ?

Sergeant.—Why, if it were seized ; for then, very likely, the magistrate would be superseded and the glorious cause suffer. You wouldn't wish that, sir.

Lieut.—No ; well—

Sergeant.—Well, then, give him the wink—just a hint that you might happen to go that way about ten o'clock to-night.

Lieut.—Very good ; and then—

Sergeant.—Then discharge your duty, sir, fearlessly, as the laws of the service require.

Lieut.—Right ; excellent, Sergeant. We have both hit on the same expedient. It requires secrecy and caution, however, to manage it properly, and knowing you to be a prudent fellow, and one of ourselves besides, I resolved to consult you. Now, you had better go yourself to the Moor this evening, see Miss Cantwell—the Rector will be at the lodge—and break the matter to her as cautiously and respectfully as possible. Observe me, if the liquor be in the house she will at once take the hint ; if it be not, she may get offended at our officiousness ; so let the circum stances best direct you how to act. When night falls go up as secretly as possible ; say I shall be there at ten o'clock precisely. Go, now, and act judiciously. [*Exit Sergeant.*]

SCENE II.

Boudoir of Miss Rebecca Cantwell. Rebecca asleep in a large arm chair by the fire. Enter Mrs. Cantwell.

Rebecca (dreaming).—Kit, Kit, my own Kit ! [*Stretching out her arms.*] Come and bring me away from this terrible place. Oh ! I am thine, thine forever.

Mrs. Cantwell —What is the meaning of this, Rebecca ? [*shaking her by the arms.*] What nonsense, Rebecca! Wake up and tell me who is this " Kit " you invoke?

Rebecca (still dreaming).—Yes, dear Kit, I know it is you—my own Kit—thine, thine forever !

Mrs. Cant. (shaking her more vigorously).—Stop—cease this folly, Rebecca! Wake up and tell me of whom you speak.

Rebecca (opening her eyes).—Oh, is it only you? Why did you disturb me? I thought it was [*sleepily*]—I thought it—was—[*Closes her eyes and is again asleep.*]

Mrs. Cant.—Very good, very good. I suspect who this Mr. Kit is. Very well, we shall see. [*Exit.*]

Rebecca (awakening slowly).—Oh! that it should be but a dream. But something whispers me that my vision will yet be realized, that I shall yet hear that voice, sweet and silvery as an angel's, saying, as it said in my dream, "Rebecca! Rebecca! come, fly with me," and looking up, I shall see in very truth the lovely face of Mr. Christopher Joice gazing down upon me with countenance illumined by the joyous light of love. [*Gets up and walks to the mirror.*] Once, when I was fresh and young, I valued lightly the love that was showered upon me. [*Gazing in the mirror.*] Now I am faded. Yes, thou tellest no falsehoods, thou reflectest but an image—an image somewhat changed for the worse, the worse. Well, I don't know; that depends on men's taste. Some like the young, and some prefer the—the lady a little more experienced than the romping girl of twenty-five.

> "Before Decay's effacing fingers
> Have swept the lines where beauty lingers,"

is an age young enough, I should imagine. A wife should be a serious matron, not a wayward, giddy child. The pretensions of young flirts nowadays are really intolerable. Marriage at sixteen! It's absolutely frightful, a disgrace to the morality of the age we live in. Generally speaking, men are fools, and as the world grows older the number increases. Kit, however, is not among that number: he has too much good sense to be running after gilded butterflies. Worth, solid worth, is his choice. Yes, I have always thought so, and last night's dream confirms me in the belief, for my dreams are ever true as the waking reality. [*Knock at the door.*] You may enter.

Maid (*entering, closely followed by Mrs. Cantwell*).—There is a messenger below from Lieutenant Joice, who desires a few moments speech with you .

Rebecca.—Show him to the library. I will come down at once. [*Exit Maid.*]

Mrs. Cant. (*passing Maid in the doorway, and entering the room*).—What is it that the girl says?

Rebecca (*carelessly*).—Some message. Nothing important, I suppose.

Mrs. Cant.—I thought I heard her mention Mr. Joice's name. I trust, Rebecca [*severely*], you will be cautious how you receive any private message from that gentleman. It is very well to be polite and even condescending to the young man, since he happens to be a convert to our religion; but anything more—no, I cannot, I will not imagine such a thing.

Rebecca.—Really, my dear sister, I must not permit you to speak in this fashion. Surely, as you have already said —surely you cannot imagine a lady of my position could for a moment entertain a serious thought of such a man.

Mrs. Cant.—Just think, Rebecca, if Baxter suspected such an intimacy!

Rebecca.—Ah, do now—do, my dear sister—do cease to tease me. How can you suspect me of such folly.

Mrs. Cant.—Suspect! and is that so very wonderful? Why, you are forever speaking of him, Rebecca, and when he is here you seem to have neither eyes nor ears for any one else; perhaps sleeping as well as waking, you are thinking of him if the truth were told.

Rebecca (coquettishly).—Oh, shame! shame, sister! Cease this folly. I am not at all in a jesting mood.

Mrs. Cant.—Well, Rebecca, all I shall say now is that your manner toward Mr. Joice is very remarkable. [*Exit.*]

Rebecca.—Perhaps so. I must be more cautious, or I shall betray myself. And now for his message. Is my dream indeed about to be realized. [*Putting her hand to her heart.*] Ah, thou wayward heart, be still. [*Exit.*]

SCENE III.

Library. Sergeant of Police standing in the centre of the room, cap in hand. Enter Rebecca.

Sergeant (bowing obsequiously).—I am the bearer of a message to you from Lieutenant Joice.

Rebecca (with much maidenly modesty).—Oh! indeed, from Mr. Joice?

Sergeant.—Yes, madam; he requests me to say he intends calling here to-night at ten o'clock precisely, and hopes nothing will be in the way. You understand me, madam? I cannot be more particular.

Rebecca (very nervously).—Oh, dear! oh, dear! you quite frighten me; what a strange message. [*Aside.*] I knew it. I felt it. My dreams are ever true.

Sergeant.—He will come very privately; no one may be the wiser, you know. He hopes all difficulties may be removed. You understand, madam; it's unnecessary to be more explicit.

(Rebecca nods and smiles.)

Sergeant.—He can't help it, madam; no, indeed. He's a victim to his feelings—he is indeed.

Rebecca.—Poor fellow.

Sergeant.—Oh! indeed, madam, if you knew the state of his feelings you'd pity him.

Rebecca.—I do pity him.

Sergeant.—To-night, madam, remember, at ten o'clock: let all be right when he comes.

Rebecca (*covering her face with her hands*).—Oh, dear! it will become so public. What will the world say of it?

Sergeant (*soothingly*).—Not at all, madam, not at all. It will all be hushed up. Don't be terrified, madam, it has happened to the best families in the kingdom; it has, indeed.

Rebecca.—Oh! but think—think how the world will speak of it; it will all be in the newspapers, too. Oh, dear! we must leave the country forever; tell him that we must fly forever. Oh, dear! how the thought terrifies me.

Sergeant.—Upon my—I beg your pardon, madam; but, faith, I can't see why you take on so for such a trifle. Sure, you know, madam, if you manage right—and you have plenty of time to put all to rights before ten o'clock —you may defy the world; and then—[*Mrs. Cantwell is heard approaching.*]

Rebecca (*slipping gold into the Sergeant's hand*).—Yes, yes; I understand. You must go quickly. Be cautious and faithful. [*Exit Sergeant by one door and Rebecca by another.*]

Scene IV.

Library. Light burning dimly. Enter Rebecca in travel-ing costume and carrying a large valise. She turns on the light and consults the clock on the mantle.

Rebecca.—It yet lacks five minutes of ten. How strange that Kit should appoint that hour, the very time at which my reverend brother is expected to return from the lodge. But, then, lovers are never prudent. No, prudence is too cold for love. Yet, should we happen to be surprised, how terrible would be the consequences! Well, there is danger in every adventure—of course, that is naturally to be anticipated—besides, danger gives a more lively interest. What of danger? Is not my heart young, and daring, and resolute in such a cause—the cause of Kit and liberty? How slowly the time passes! [*Again glancing toward the clock.*] Ah! there is my poor little canary [*going over to the cage*] sleeping on its perch with its little head under its wing. It has been caged up, like myself, for years, and like myself, has borne its imprisonment with resignation—no, not resignation, with patience—because there was no alternative. Well, if the dear bird found the door of its cage opened by some good angel, would it not fly away and be free? To be sure it would. Yes, and I must give it liberty, too. At the moment when my own long looked for happiness is about to be realized, I must not be niggardly of my favors. No, three hearts shall beat happily on the morrow. [*Opens the door of the cage. Clock strikes ten. Rebecca places her hand on her heart and listens in evident agitation. As the last stroke dies away, she seats herself at the window. Enter Maid and Lieutenant Joice in a stealthy and secret manner.*]

Maid.—Ah! she is here. Lieutenant Joice, Miss Cantwell.

(*Rebecca rises and extends her hand.*)

Lieut. J. (*advancing and pressing her hand affectionately*). —Oh! my dear Miss Cantwell, can you—say—can you pardon this—

Rebecca.—Oh, dear, dear. I fear I shall never be able to—

Lieut. J.—Don't be terrified, Miss Cantwell. Be composed; it's quite a common thing.

Rebecca.—Oh, I know that, my dear Kit; but I am naturally so nervous, so excitable.

Lieut. J.—There is no cause, I assure you, Miss Cantwell, for this excitement.

Rebecca (sinks sobbing into a chair).—Oh, what will the world say?

Lieut. J.—The world! What has the world to do with it?

Rebecca.—Oh, think of the newspapers and the scandal mongers.

Lieut. J.—Mere folly, my dear Miss Cantwell. You agitate yourself quite too much for such a trifle. Be calm, do, now; it will all be over in a few minutes.

Rebecca (with sudden calmness).—I am perfectly resigned.

Lieut. J. (encouragingly).—Trust all to me.

Rebecca.—Perhaps I am too confiding, my dear Kit. I feel I have not done right in meeting you here. But fate would have it so—our destiny is not in our own hands.

Lieut. J. (perplexed).—Why, my dear Miss Cantwell, I fear I cannot well understand the cause of your apprehensions. Have you had everything arranged as the Sergeant intimated?

Rebecca.—Everything.

Lieut. J.—There is nothing to dread, is there?

Rebecca (aside).—What a question. No, nothing, I believe.

Lieut. J.—Well, and why do you appear so terrified?

Rebecca (becoming agitated).—Don't know; woman's heart is fearful—the weakness of our sex, perhaps. It is such a dreadful step to take, you know.

Lieut. J.—Dreadful step! [*Aside.*] What the mischief does the woman mean?

Rebecca.—You men think little of it, perhaps; but is all ready? [*Aside.*] Why is he so cold and apathetic? This lelay is dangerous. My brother may return at any moment. Have you brought any one to assist? I mean to—

Lieut. J.—To assist? Yes; the men are in waiting beyond there among the trees.

Rebecca (*taking up the valise and setting it on the window-sill*).—Well then, call one of them, and have him take this to the carriage. I intrust my life and my honor to you, Kit. I have never concealed my love from you—never; and, oh! remember, Kit, remember in after years the sacrifices I have made for you this night; that I am leaving all that is near and dear to me in this world—home, friends, kindred, and country perhaps—to be thine—thine forever. [*Loud knocking is heard.*] But, what's that? Knocking at the hall door. Kit! Kit! that's my brother's knock. Oh! let us fly—fly while there is yet time.

Lieut. J. (*in utter amazement*).—Fly! What? You must have mistaken—

Rebecca.—Mistaken! Mr. Joice, you surely—you came here to—

Lieut. J.—To make a seizure. [*Rebecca screams and falls fainting on the floor. Joice picks her up and lays her on a sofa. He is bending over her untying her bonnet, when the door is burst violently open, and Rev. Baxter Cantwell enters. He rushes at Joice, and, seizing a large dusting brush, deals him a heavy blow that fells him to the floor.*]

Rev. B. Cant. (*flourishing the brush*).—Villain! villain! what means this outrage? [*Enters Mrs. Cant. and Maid.*]

Lieut. J. (*raising his arm to protect his head*).—It's all a mistake.

Mrs. Cant.—Mistake! Wretch! Miscreant! Is that

the evidence of a mistake? [*Points to valise, which has been knocked off the window and lies on the floor burst open.*]

Rev. Cant.—Low, mean, unprincipled, vile wretch. [*Rushing at Joice, who scrambles to his feet.*] Is this the reward you offer us for all our kindness?

Lieut. J.—It's only a mistake. I wished to save you the disgrace of a public exposure; but now [*blowing a small whistle*]—now I shall treat you with as little civility as your conduct deserves.

(*Sergeant and policemen tumble in precipitately through the window.*)

Rev. Cant.—Merciful powers! What does all this mean? Is my house to be polluted by this fellow and his men! Villain! do you dare me to my face—do you? Are you re-solved to carry her off by brute force—are you?

Lieut. J.—I come to carry off your smuggled liquor—not your sister; and only that I respect your calling more than you yourself have done to-night, I should arrest you for obstructing me—a King's officer—in the discharge of my duty. Sergeant, proceed to the cellar and make the seizure.

Rev. Cant. (*seizing a blunderbuss from the corner*).—Hold! hold! Countermand that order, or—[*Raises the blunderbuss to a level with the officer's heart.*]

Lieut. J.—I shall do my duty. Men, guard the room. [*Policeman seizes the blunderbuss and wrests it from the hands of Rev. Cantwell. Another intercepts Mrs. Cantwell as she is about to leave the room for assistance. Maid is busy with Miss Rebecca.*] Sergeant, take command! This gen-tleman is your prisoner, at least till I return from the cel-lar. [*Exit Lieutenant, with remainder of the men. If there be but three, one should remain with the Sergeant, and two accompany the Lieutenant. If more, let two remain with the Sergeant, and the rest go with the Lieutenant.*]

Scene V.

Same as before. Re-enter Lieutenant, with men carrying two kegs.

Lieut. J.—Now, sir, you are at liberty. Should I here-after think it necessary to prosecute you for obstruction, you can be easily found. I have received a written infor-mation of two casks of unpermitted liquor having been deposited in your cellar, reverend sir, by one James Gal-linach, of Lough Devnish, and, accordingly, have seized these two casks, believing them to be the same, and shall detain them till such time as my inspector may call upon you, sir, in open court, to show cause why you may not be fined in the penalty of one hundred pounds sterling for attempting to defraud his Majesty's revenue. I came here, reverend sir, to discharge my duty, and however painful it may have been to me under the circumstances, yet was I bound to execute it faithfully or lose my commission. Miss Cantwell will doubtless explain to you, when she re-covers from the effects of this very disagreeable mistake, how friendly were my intentions in this unlucky affair. As to the violence offered myself personally, I pardon it ; for the rest, the law must take its course. [*To his men.*] Take up the liquor and proceed to your quarters. [*Exit Lieutenant, Sergeant, and men. Rebecca rises with difficulty and, supported by the Maid, glides unobserved from the room.*]

Mrs. Cant.—Well, sir, this is a pretty pickle the Rector's family has gotten into, eh, isn't it ?

Rev. Cant.—It's painful to flesh and blood, my dear, but we must bear it with patience and resignation

Mrs. Cant.—Very good, sir; and I presume you will, after this night, continue to commit smugglers to jail?

Rev. Cant.—You speak bitterly, my dear. It is right that we should do our duty under all circumstances.

[CURTAIN.]

ESTHER WILSON BROWN.

SIGNING THE PLEDGE.

CHARACTERS.

ARTHUR	ED.	WALTER.
WILL.	LOUIS.	MR. BLAKE.

SCENE.—*Parlor. Arthur seated at the table writing in a book. Enter Walter.*

Arthur.—I'm glad you've come; you're the very boy I wanted to see.

Walter.—Well, that's lucky, for you're the very chap I'm after. Can you go out with me this evening?

Arthur.—Sit down, Walter. No, I was in hopes you could spend the evening with me. Our society, of which I am secretary, meets here this evening.

Walter.—Society! why, I thought you were not going to join the "Wild Rangers."

Arthur.—No, I should think not, the name is enough for me, I mean the "Blue Ribbon Society."

Walter.—That sounds like a girls' society. What is it for? What do you do?

Arthur.—It is to help the boys grow up to be sober, honest, industrious men. Don't you want to join it?

Walter.—I don't know. I expect to grow up to be a sober, honest, and industrious man.

(*A knock at the door. Arthur opens it. Enter Ed, Louis and Will.*)

Arthur.—Take seats boys, you are just in time. I am trying to persuade Walter to join us.

Louis.—I stopped to see you about it to-day, but you were not at home.

Walter.—I wish some of you would tell me what it is. Is there any fun in it?

Will.—There are no larks in it, as the "Wild Rangers" have, if that is what you mean by fun.

Ed.—Yes, they will have so much fun the police will catch them some night.

Walter.—Well! I must be off down the street. Are you going to tell me what you do in your "Blue Ribbon Society"?

Arthur.—All you will have to do is to sign the pledge never to touch, taste, or handle intoxicating liquors.

Walter (contemptuously).—Oh! It's a temperance society. No, I thank you, I don't join anything of that sort.

Louis.—Why not?

Walter.—Oh!—because—Well! I don't want to. I intend to drink or let it alone, just as I please. Father says he doesn't believe in signing a pledge—that a man should have manliness enough about him to stop before he drinks too much.

Will.—What do you mean by too much?

Walter.—Why, getting drunk, staggering along the streets, and all that sort of thing.

Will.—Do you suppose a man ever intends doing that when he commences drinking?

Walter.—No; but men should have sense enough to stop before they go so far.

Will.—Perhaps they can't stop.

Walter.—I wouldn't give much for a man that has not will power enough to stop what he knows is injuring him.

Ed.—My father says that these moderate drinkers do more harm than all the drunkards put together. There isn't more than one man out of ten that can drink or let it alone. And because he can drink a little and stop, the other nine think they can do the same. But they find their mistake when it is too late.

(*Mr. Blake comes in while Ed. is speaking, and stands listening, unseen by the boys.*)

Mr. Blake (stepping forward).—Bravo! Edward, I am glad to hear you say that. Boys, I have been listening to your conversation, and I should like to relate an experience of my own for Walter's benefit, if you have time to hear it.

Walter.—Certainly, Mr. Blake. I shall be glad to listen.

Mr. Blake (taking a chair).—When I was about eighteen years of age a temperance pledge was introduced in our Sunday-school. Several of my friends signed it, but I, like Walter, thought it unmanly to sign a pledge. I had one very dear friend, Harry North, who wished to sign it. I knew if he signed it, it would be for life, for he always kept his word; so I persuaded him not to do it, told him he could abstain from drinking just as well without it. The years rolled round; we went together to college, and were almost inseparable. Many merry times did we have together, and often when we would have our little champagne suppers with our friends, I would congratulate Harry that he had not signed the pledge, or it would have spoiled our fun.

I attained my majority while at college and celebrated the event by giving a party to our club. [*Speaking with emotion.*] And oh! my dear boys, may none of you ever have cause to look back to your twenty-first birthday with as sad a heart as I do to-night. After all these years the scene is as fresh in my memory as though it had occurred yesterday. I, of course, treated the boys to liquors. I noticed that Harry drank more than the one or two glasses to which he had limited himself, and that when we left the club rooms he was excited. On our way home he and another student were arguing about some trivial matter, and when they reached a certain saloon, insisted upon going in. Boys, I cannot go into the details of that scene. Harry, under the influence of the liquor I had furnished him, drew a pistol and shot one whom he had always respected. Then, frantic at the terrible deed he had committed, blew out his own brains before any one could interfere. It was a fearful blow to me. I felt that I was to blame for his death. And oh! the agony that I endured for weeks and months after my friend was buried forever from my sight! All this suffering was due to what I considered an innocent glass of liquor. Boys, there is danger in it all. There is no safety except in total abstinence. My terrible experience has made me feel that I must warn every one whom my voice can reach of the deadly evil that lurks in the sparkling glass.

Walter.—I thank you deeply for telling me this sad tale. I shall never want to look at liquor again. Boys, I will sign your pledge, and that means I shall be a life member.

(*Boys all rise. Arthur hands him a pen and the book. He writes his name. Mr. Blake takes his hand.*)

Mr. Blake (*earnestly*).—I pray that by your resolve, many may be saved from a wrecked and ruined life. And may each of you, both by precept and example, do all in your power to promote the principle of total abstinence in our land.

[CURTAIN.]

ELLA H. CLEMENT.

JOE FLEMING'S THANKSGIVING.

(*Adapted.*)

CHARACTERS.

JOE FLEMING, poor, but energetic.   · NELLIE FLEMING, his wife.

SCENE.—*A modestly furnished living room.   Table in centre spread with tea service.   Cradle at left, by which Nellie Fleming is discovered sitting.   Time, evening.*

Nellie.—Dear, dear me!   What a long, miserable Thansgiving day I have spent, with nobody to talk to but baby.   And now it is past seven o'clock, and Joe has not come home yet.   How hard he does work at that office, to be sure.   Couldn't rest even on Thanksgiving, but must be off to town early and must stay in town late; and when he comes home its precious little time he has to talk with me, isn't it, baby dear?   Papa has so much writing to do, dearest, hasn't he?   See how baby laughs, as if he understood every word.   Well, it's all for you, little one.   I'm sure he never worked so hard until you were born.   Do you know what I said to him?   No, of course you don't; how could you?   Well, I said to him, "Joe, we ought to lay up a little money for baby's sake!"   "So we ought, dear," said papa, "and so we will," and then papa took extra writing from the law stationer, which he does at night, and mamma spent her leisure hours writing sketches for a story paper, and the money began to come in, and the little pile grew and grew until at last we had a hundred dollars saved. And then, baby, dear, what did mamma want papa to do with it? She wanted him to speculate, didn't she? And he wouldn't. "No," he said, "small gains and sure, that's my motto." O baby, dear! if we were only rich. If you could but get a college education and go abroad, and take your place with the wealthy and honored of the land!

(*Footsteps are heard outside R. Nellie rises suddenly and the next instant Joe Fleming bursts into the room in an excited manner.*

Nellie.—O Joe! I'm so glad you've come. You don't know what a dull day—what a miserable Thanksgiving I have had—but what's the matter, dear? What has happened?

Joe (dropping into a chair).—What do you guess, pet?

Nellie.—Your salary has been raised?

Joe.—Better than that!

Nellie.—My last story has been accepted!

Joe.—Better than that!

Nellie.—I give it up. O Joe! tell me at once. What is it?

Joe.—Cousin Frank is dead and he has left me all his money.

Nellie (bewildered).—Cousin Frank!

Joe.—That eccentric old fellow out in Peoria, my third cousin. He disinherited his daughter because she didn't marry to suit him; made at least half a dozen wills and burned them all except one bearing a codicil that makes the fortune mine. Hurrah! We're rich people at last pet! Eighty thousand dollars at least! Three cheers! and give them with a will!

Nellie.—O Joe! you'll frighten baby and make him cry

Joe.—Bother baby! Let him cry a little; it is good for his lungs. We can have a patent perambulator now, and a nursery fitted up with all the modern conveniences. Eh! [*Getting up and going over toward cradle.*] That's something worth bawling for, isn't it, little chubby cheeks! This is indeed a day for thanksgiving.

Nellie.—O Joe! And then we can have Uncle Thomas and Aunt Mary to live with us.

Joe.—Uncle Tom and Aunt Mary! What should they live with us for?

Nellie.—But Joe, they are so poor!

Joe.—There are a great many poor people in the world. Nell.

Nellie.—And Cousin Will's education. We can help him through college now.

Joe.—Well, I'd like to know what business it is of ours to help Will Carey through college? Nobody helped me through college, I know! If we're going to divide our money with all creation, there soon will be an end of our riches.

(*Nellie looks pained but says nothing.*)

Joe (continuing).—We'll have a big house in town pet, and—

Nellie—O Joe! I would much rather live in the country.

Joe.—I wouldn't then! The city for me!

Nellie.—Yes, but Joe—

Joe.—Mrs. Fleming you will please remember that the money is mine, not yours.

(*Nellie bites her lips and looks hurt.*)

Joe (continuing).—Good thing for me that Mary Potter

threw herself away on that drunken fellow. [*Sits down at table.*] It's an ill wind that blows nobody good.

Nellie (going over and sitting opposite to him).—But Joe you will surely make the poor girl an allowance!

Joe.—Make her an allowance! I shall do nothing of the kind. Why should I?

Nellie.—Because the money should rightfully be hers; because she is deprived of it by a mere caprice of her father; because we are neither more nor less than thieves if we take it from her!

Joe.—Nell, you're a fool! Do look at things from a business point of view. The money is ours!

Nellie.—But it will be no blessing to us if come by wrongfully.

Joe.—I am the best judge of that Mrs. Fleming!

(*Nellie bursts into tears.*)

Nellie (speaking between her sobs).—Joe, you never spoke to me so unkindly before!

Joe.—Didn't I? Well you never made such a dunce of yourself before!

Nellie (still sobbing).—O don't talk like that Joe; you'll break my heart. I'm sure I only told you what I thought was right, and if you will consider for a while I know you will come to my way of thinking. Don't let us get selfish because we are rich, dear!

Joe.—I'm not selfish; and I don't intend to be selfish, but I'm not going to divide up what little we have with all our relatives; so Mrs. Fleming, you can just hold your tongue on that subject, and I will thank you to pour out my tea. The supper must be stone cold by this time, as it is!

Nellie.—O Joe, how cross you are! I wish the money

was all at the bottom of the sea. We were much happier before we ever heard of it. [*Beginning to pour out tea.*]

Joe.—There, there now. That's nice kind of talk, I must say! Wish it was all at the bottom of the sea, do you? A woman's logic, and no mistake. [*Turning up his plate.*] What's this, a letter? I say, Nell, why didn't you tell me this was here?

Nellie (looking up).—What, Joe? O the letter! Yes, I forgot. It came this morning, soon after you left. I put it there so you would be sure to get it. The news of the fortune drove it quite out of my head.

Joe (looking at envelope).—From Davis & Brown, Cousin Frank's lawyers [*breaking the seal*]. Vigilant, wide-awake fellows they are, too! I think I shall continue to employ them! [*Begins reading:*] " Peoria, November 25th. Mr. Joseph Fleming, Dear Sir : We regret to have to inform you—" Eh? How—why! What's this! The deuce! [*Lets letter fall from his hands and sits staring blankly at Nellie.*]

Nellie.—O Joe ! What is the matter? What in the world has happened ?

Joe.—What is the matter? Matter enough, I'm sure. Instead of being rich we're not a cent better off than we were yesterday !

Nellie.—You don't mean it?

Joe.—Don't I though! [*Handing her the letter.*] There take it, and read for yourself! They've found a new will, dated ten days later than any other document, and every cent is left to Cousin Frank's daughter, Mary—the undutiful girl who married against her father's wishes.

Nellie (looking over the letter while Joe gets up and takes two or three nervous turns up and down the stage).—And so **we are poor again! And we couldn't help anybody if we** wanted to; and baby can't have a patent perambulator and a nursery; and we can't afford to live in the city. O my, how the air castles are tumbling! And O my, Joe, dear, how I rejoice in their destruction.   I was just beginning to think that I had no cause for thanks at all, because I was afraid this money was taking your love from me and baby, but now—

Joe.—But now, darling, we will give thanks together. Do you know, pet, I am very glad too! I don't think I should make a good millionaire.   I was becoming grasping already, and I felt as though the whole world were in league to cheat me.   I am rich enough with you and baby, and I can carve out a fortune for myself.   This will teach us a lesson, dear.   It will teach us to be thankful for the blessings we have, and to be content.   After all God knows what is best for us!

[CURTAIN.]

CHARLES STOKES WAYNE.